"A valuable addition to the literature on the topic, particularly for managers and senior contributors . . . *Kill It with Fire* is a useful and highly readable guide to solving these problems by leveraging the organization—the system around the system."

—Laura Nolan, USENIX

"Modernizing legacy systems is an increasingly common task for software developers. *Kill It with Fire* guides you through the ins and outs of these endeavors in an engaging way, diving into both the technical and social aspects that are crucial to making you successful when undertaking modernization projects."

–Damian Schenkelman, Principal Engineer, Auth0

"Incredibly well timed. For those alarmed by the provocative title, rest assured the only thing Bellotti advocates torching is the notion of torching itself. And while the book is written for technical leadership, her wisdom is something many nontechnical government leaders need to hear right now, lest they fall prey to the gaggle of advisers saying things like 'we just need to get them off the mainframe.' . . . Bellotti's book could not have come at a better time, and while there are other factors in this equation, she outlines some of the most important."

—Jennifer Pahlka, Medium's OneZero

"A business book that's actually not a waste of time."

—David Youd, YouTuber and Goodreads Librarian

"A most excellent book for both engineers and managers alike."

—Michael Simons, @rotnroll666, Programmer

KILL IT WITH FIRE

MANAGE AGING COMPUTER SYSTEMS (AND FUTURE-PROOF MODERN ONES)

by MARIANNE BELLOTTI

no starch press

San Francisco

Printed in the United States of America

Second printing

26 25 24 23 22   2 3 4 5 6

ISBN-13: 978-1-7185-0118-8 (print)
ISBN-13: 978-1-7185-0119-5 (ebook)

Publisher: William Pollock
Executive Editor: Barbara Yien
Production Editor: Katrina Taylor
Developmental Editor: Jill Franklin
Cover Design: Octopod Studios
Interior Design: Maureen Forys, Happenstance Type-O-Rama
Copyeditor: Kim Wimpsett
Compositor: Happenstance Type-O-Rama
Proofreader: James Fraleigh

For information on distribution, bulk sales, corporate sales, or translations, please contact No Starch Press, Inc. directly at info@nostarch.com or:

No Starch Press, Inc.
245 8th Street, San Francisco, CA 94103
phone: 1-415-863-9900
www.nostarch.com

Library of Congress Control Number: 2020950272

[S]

*For my father, who kept the 360 system
manual in our attic "just in case."*

About the Author

Marianne Bellotti has worked as a software engineer for over 15 years. She built data infrastructure for the United Nations to help humanitarian organizations share crisis data worldwide and spent three and a half years running incident response for the United States Digital Service. While in government, she found success applying organizational change management techniques to the problem of modernizing legacy software systems. More recently, she was in charge of Platform Services at Auth0. She currently runs Identity and Access Control at Rebellion Defense.

BRIEF CONTENTS

CONTENTS IN DETAIL

We build our computer systems the way we build our cities: over time, without a plan, on top of ruins.

—ELLEN ULLMAN

INTRODUCTION

I n 1975, renowned physicist David L. Goodstein published his book *States of Matter* with the following introduction:

> *Ludwig Boltzmann, who spent much of his life studying statistical mechanics, died in 1906, by his own hand. Paul Ehrenfest, carrying on the work, died similarly in 1933. Now it is our turn to study statistical mechanics.*

This is a book about how to run legacy modernizations, a topic many software engineers regard as slow-moving career suicide, if not the prologue to a literal one. This book is for people who work at large organizations with aging technology, but it is also a book for people who work at small startups still building their technology. Restoring legacy systems to operational excellence is ultimately about resuscitating an iterative development process so that the systems are being maintained and evolving as time goes on.

Most of the advice in this book can just as easily be used for building new technology, but legacy systems hold a special place in my heart. I spent the first 10 years of my professional career traveling around the world, looking for work in applied anthropology while programming computers for fun on the side. I knew how to program because my father was a computer programmer, and I grew up in a house filled with computers at a time when that was rare.

I never became the swashbuckling international aid worker I imagined myself to be, but I ended up finding my applied anthropology work in legacy modernizations. Like pottery sherds, old computer programs are artifacts of human thought. There's so much you can tell about an organization's past by looking at its code.

To understand legacy systems, you have to be able to define how the original requirements were determined. You have to excavate an entire thought process and figure out what the trade-offs look like now that the options are different.

Simply being old is not enough to make something legacy. The subtext behind the phrase *legacy technology* is that it's also bad, barely functioning maybe, but legacy technology exists only if it is successful. These old programs are perhaps less efficient than they were before, but technology that isn't used doesn't survive decades.

We are past the point where all technical conversations and knowledge sharing can be about building new things. We have too many old things. People from my father's generation wrote a lot of programs, and every year they are shocked by how much of their work survives, still running in a production system somewhere. My generation has programmed exponentially more, infecting every aspect of life with a computer chip and some runtime instructions. We will be similarly shocked when those systems are still in place 30, 40, or 50 years from now.

Because we don't talk about modernizing old tech, organizations fall into the same traps over and over again. Failure is predictable because so many software engineers think the conversations about modernizing legacy technology are not relevant to their careers. Some of them are honestly surprised to find out that COBOL still runs much of the financial sector, that the majority of the web is still written in PHP, or that people are still looking to hire software engineers with ActionScript, Flash, and Visual Basic skills.

Failure can be so predictable that after a year or two of doing this work, I found that with a little basic information about the technology deployed, I could predict a series of problems the organization was facing and how its solutions had failed. Occasionally, I would perform this parlor trick for the amusement of other engineers and the advancement of my career, including once during a job interview at the *New York Times*.

When I left government to go back to the private sector, I discovered that the same techniques that had worked for old systems also worked really well with relatively new systems. I moved to a six-year-old company and did legacy modernization work. Then I moved to a six-month-old company and still did legacy modernization work. At one point, exasperated, I complained to my boss, "Why am I running a legacy modernization on a three-month-old system?" To which he retorted, "Serves you right for not showing up three months ago."

That being said, there is little downside to maintaining all systems as if they are legacy systems. It is easy to build things, but it is difficult to rethink them once they are in place. Legacy modernizations are hard not because they are technically hard—the problems and the solutions are usually well understood—it's the people side of the modernization effort that is hard. Getting the time and resources to actually implement the change, building an appetite for change to happen and keeping that momentum, managing the intra-organizational communication necessary to move a system that any number of other systems connect to or rely upon—those things are hard.

And yet, as an industry, we do not talk about these challenges. We assume the sun, moon, stars, and the board of directors will all magically reconfigure themselves around the right technical answer simply because it's the right technical answer. We are horrified to discover that most people do not actually care how healthy a piece of technology is as long as it performs the function they need it to with a reasonable degree of accuracy in a timeframe that doesn't exhaust their patience. In technology, "good enough" reigns supreme.

In trying to explain how to approach a legacy modernization, I first go back and explore how technology changes over time. Chapters 1 and 2 both explore the mechanics of computing trends and best practices: How did we settle on the technology that is legacy today, and what can we learn from that process to guide our modernization plans?

In Chapter 3, I discuss the three broad problems that make organizations feel like they need to modernize: technical debt, performance issues, and system stability. I give an example of each type of problem on a real (though anonymous) system and how the plan to modernize it might come together.

Chapter 4 discusses why legacy modernization is so hard and fails so often. I address the great myth of cross-platform compatibility and the role of abstraction in manipulating what we see as easy or hard.

Chapter 5 talks about the most critical feature of any legacy modernization: momentum. How do you get it, and how do you keep it? I outline a whole series of conditions—some of them momentum killers, some of them momentum growers.

Chapter 6 deals with coming into a modernization project that has already started and how to fix the most common problems that might be stalling it.

Chapter 7 provides as thorough of an overview as possible into design thinking and how we can use design to direct and ultimately improve the outcomes of technical conversations.

Chapter 8 is all about breaking stuff and the value of not being afraid of failure. I explore how chaos testing complements legacy modernization and how to work with an organization where the suggestion that you should break things on purpose might seem like a bridge too far.

Chapter 9 discusses why success is not as obvious or self-evident as you might assume and how to define criteria to determine when a project is finished.

Finally, Chapter 10 lays out strategies to keep you from ever having to do a modernization on the same system again. How do you know if your software is maintainable? What can you do if it is not?

The language in this book is deliberate. I use the term *organization* instead of *company* or *business*. The vast majority of my work experience in this space is with governments and nonprofits, but legacy is everywhere. The organizations that need to build and maintain good technology are not exclusively in the private sector. The US federal government is one of the single largest producers of technology, for example. The conversation about legacy systems crosses from businesses to governments to hospitals to nonprofits. For that reason, when I mention the "business" side of the organization, I mean that in terms of the mission-focused components that engineering is building technology to support. An organization doesn't have to make a profit to have a business side.

Throughout the book, I use the word *system* to refer to a grouping of technologies that work together for a common set of tasks. System is a troublesome word in technology conversations as it seems you can never find a group of engineers who agree where its boundaries are. For my purposes, though, that vagueness is beneficial. It allows me to talk about legacy modernizations in general.

To describe parts of a system, I frequently use the words *component* or occasionally *service*. While many of the techniques in this book are applicable to any type of technology, examples and discussions are heavily slanted toward software engineering and web-based development in particular. I couldn't write a book about legacy systems without mainframes, data centers, and old operating systems, but most of my experience is with upgrading these systems to more internet-friendly options, and this book reflects that. I look forward to technologists with other backgrounds supplementing the material in this book with essays on whether my advice also applies to them.

My sincere hope is that as you read this, you find inspiration for your own technical projects, regardless of the age of your technology. I've tried my best to pack as many resources, exercises, and frameworks into this book as possible, to be as detailed as possible, and to ground as many assertions with real-world stories as I can.

We are reaching a tipping point with legacy systems. The generation that built the oldest of them is gradually dying off, and we are piling more and more layers of society on top of these old, largely undocumented and unmaintained computer programs. While I don't believe society is going to crumble at our feet over it, there's a lot of good, interesting work for people willing to jump in.

TIME IS A FLAT CIRCLE

In the summer of 2016, I found myself sitting in front of the weirdest system I had ever encountered as a software engineer. There was a fairly banal web application written in Java that was connecting to what I would eventually figure out was a mainframe. The mainframe itself wasn't the weird part. When you venture into the world of legacy modernization, you quickly realize that mainframes are still *everywhere*—in banks, in government, buried deep in the foundation of civil society. Having a web application send requests to a mainframe wasn't so weird. I had a hard time accepting that a technology designed for bulk transactions would respond quickly enough to meet the demands of a website at a reasonable scale, but despite my concerns, it did appear to be doing okay.

No, what was weird was that the mainframe in question was from the 1960s and storing data on magnetic tape. There was no way *that* mainframe could respond quickly enough, so when I saw this on the architecture diagrams, I focused on a group of mysterious machines that were sitting in the middle; a modern web application was on one side and an ancient mainframe on the other.

The only information I had about this cluster of machines was the acronym the organization used for it. Nobody on the engineering teams I was working with seemed to know what the machines did. It took a lot of digging through several decades of documentation before I figured out what they were: *Unisys ClearPath Dorados*. In other words, they were more mainframes, newer ones, that were effectively configured like a cache in front of the old mainframe. That was how 60-year-old code was responding fast enough to serve requests from the modern internet. The organization had a new machine sitting in between that was storing a temporary copy of the relevant data. About once a week, the new mainframes would request an update from the older mainframe.

When I asked an engineer who worked on this system what he thought about this arrangement, he said something that has stuck with me ever since and ultimately changed my understanding of modernizing legacy computer systems: "Well, how is the cloud any different from old time-sharing schemes on mainframes?"

The answer is that it isn't really. Both of these approaches charge you for time spent on shared resources maintained by a much larger institution. You are connecting over the same lines of communication, sometimes with the same protocols. The client/server model is virtually the same; only the interfaces and programming languages are different. On this point, the engineer added another interesting observation: "We started with thin-client mainframe green-screen terminal applications, then they wanted us to migrate to fat clients on PCs, now they want APIs with thin clients again."

The first mistake software engineers make with legacy modernization is assuming technical advancement is linear. With that frame of mind, anything built in older design patterns or with an older architectural philosophy is inferior to newer options. Improving the performance of an old system is just a matter of rearranging it to a new pattern.

My experiences dealing with Frankenstein systems like the one described taught me that progress in technology is not linear. It's cyclical.

We advance, but we advance slowly, while moving tangentially. We abandon patterns only to reinvent them later and sell them as completely new.

Technology advances not by building on what came before, but by *pivoting* from it. We take core concepts from what exists already and modify them to address a gap in the market; then we optimize around filling in that gap until that optimization has aggregated all the people and use cases not covered by the new tech into its own distinct market that another "advancement" will capture.

In other words, the arms race around data centers left smaller organizations behind and created a demand for the commercial cloud. Optimizing the cloud for customization and control created the market for managed platforms and eventually serverless computing. The serverless model will feed its consumers more and more development along its most appealing features until the edge cases where serverless approaches don't quite fit start to find common ground among each other. Then a new product will come out that will address those needs.

Leveraging What Came Before

Most people realize that technology can be invented and not become popular until much later, but they typically attribute this effect to the lack of vision of the inventor or deficiencies of skills within the marketing department or the maturity level of the technology itself.

Economists have a different explanation for adoption rates of new technology. They typically describe it as the contrast between alignable and nonalignable differences. *Alignable differences* are those for which the consumer has a reference point. For example, *this* car is faster than *that* car, or *this* phone has a better camera than *that* phone.

Nonalignable differences are characteristics that are wholly unique and innovative; there are no reference points with which to compare. You might assume that nonalignable differences are more appealing to potential consumers. After all, there's no competition! You're doing things differently from everyone else. But when it comes time to make a purchasing decision, if there is no comparison, there is no clear sense of value. How does one judge the worth of something—and therefore estimate the trade-offs of buying it at a particular price—that has no equivalent? For a nonalignable difference to make an impact, the estimated value it produces has to be greater than all the alignable differences and all the other nonalignable differences put together.[1]

Consumers just aren't confident about having to do such guesswork.[2] It increases the risk of buyer's remorse, and reasoning about needs and utility makes consumers uncomfortable. Therefore, products of all kinds differentiate themselves on the market by finding specific characteristics that can be labeled as different from characteristics of existing solutions. This pushes technology into cycles. People do not get exactly the same experience from the same products. As a company iterates to improve a certain characteristic of the product, it ultimately makes the product less desirable for the group of existing customers. Companies do this with the hope that a larger group of new customers will make that loss irrelevant.

Most of the time this gradual optimization only creates annoyances that play themselves out over social media and eventually die down. Occasionally, there are enough people who have experienced a loss in utility from the optimization that they themselves become a potential market to be captured. That includes consumers who never bought the product in the first place but would have if it had been optimized in some other way. Leveraging alignable differences is pushing the product

[1] Shi Zhang and Arthur B. Markman, "Overcoming the Early Entrant Advantage: The Role of Alignable and Nonalignable Differences," *Journal of Marketing Research* 35, no. 4 (1998): 413–426, *https://www.jstor.org/stable/3152161*.

[2] John T. Gourville and Dilip Soman, "Overchoice and Assortment Type: When and Why Variety Backfires," *Marketing Science* 24, no. 3 (2005): 382–395, *https://www.jstor.org/stable/40056969*.

further away from what those consumers want to buy, but creating an opportunity for another company to figure out.

Consider the following: Is it better to have a small cellphone or a large cellphone?

The world's first commercially available cellphone was Motorola's DynaTAC 800. It was the big brick phone now used to signal the 1980s in satirical pieces. More than 10 inches tall, it wasn't the sort of thing one could easily carry around in a pocket. Obviously, market demands would push cellphones to grow smaller. By 1994, IBM's Simon had gotten them down to 8 inches tall and added the industry's first attempt at smart features such as sending faxes and emails, maintaining a calendar, keeping notes, reading the news, and viewing stock prices. Despite those impressive advancements, the Simon was quickly made irrelevant by the flip phone, which took the 8-inch size and literally folded it in half, making it similar in size to the average width and the depth of a pants pocket.[3] Companies went from selling tens of thousands to millions of devices.

I was in high school during this time, and despite the ubiquity of them now, a cellphone was not something a kid in the 1990s would have considered a worthwhile purchase. I had only one friend who had a cellphone, and it served two primary functions for him: something for when his car broke down driving back and forth to his part-time job at Taco Bell, and playing a grayscale version of *Snake* during class. For me and my peers, though, we were just as likely to run into the people we might want to call in the hallway between classes, or we could communicate with them through other means that our parents paid for. Texting was not a medium we considered for the cellphone. Pagers worked just as well.

In fact, a Pew Research study revealed that *landlines* were still the communication medium of choice for American teenagers almost a

---

[3.] Jan Diehm and Amber Thomas, "Women's Pockets Are Inferior," The Pudding, August 2018, *https://pudding.cool/2018/08/pockets/*.

decade later in 2009.[4] More than half of teenagers had never even sent a text message. By this point, the iPhone had been on the market for two years, and it was in its third iteration. A year later, a follow-up report from Pew painted a completely different picture: cellphone use in the United States was rapidly growing among teenagers, overtaking all other communication options.[5]

What happened?

An internet meme goes around every now and again that pegs the pivot point on cellphone size at around 2005 with the words "Here we realize we can see porn in the mobile." In reality, screen sizes varied up until 2010 with plenty of options from the all-encompassing touch screen look to more modest interfaces with physical keyboards that were optimized for business use cases. Teenagers were lingering as an underserved market until screen size started to increase and cameras became more of a first-class feature of phones. What teenagers wanted to use cellphones for was sharing pictures and videos with each other.[6] Once it became clear there was a market to capture by selling phones as entertainment devices, cellphones abruptly stopped shrinking and started growing. Innovations around resolution, display, and camera quality accelerated.

It's tempting to look at these trends and assume the technology simply matured to the point where it was able to find and seize its market. But the data doesn't actually bear that out. Nokia's N95 offered a

---

[4.] Amanda Lenhart, "Teens and Mobile Phones Over the Past Five Years: Pew Internet Looks Back," Pew Research Center's Internet & American Life Project, August 19, 2009, https://www.pewresearch.org/internet/2009/08/19/teens-and-mobile-phones-over-the-past-five-years-pew-internet-looks-back/.

[5.] Amanda Lenhart, Rich Ling, Scott Campbell, and Kristen Purcell, "Teens and Mobile Phones," Pew Research Center's Internet & American Life Project, April 20, 2010, https://www.pewresearch.org/internet/2010/04/20/teens-and-mobile-phones/.

[6.] Ibid.

5-megapixel (MP) camera in 2007. Shortly thereafter, the first-generation iPhone came out with a 2MP camera, and the HTC Dream was released in 2008 with 3.15MP camera. In 2010, the iPhone and HTC would debut front-facing cameras with 0.3MP and 1.3MP, respectively. The technology on the market wasn't getting better; it was briefly getting worse.[7]

Simply producing a cellphone that was geared toward teenagers in the 1990s or the early 2000s would not have led to an explosion of growth. Teenagers had no strong reference point for cellphones. From their viewpoint, there were no alignable differences attractive enough to justify the expense. It was only once their parents' devices became prevalent in cultural references and everyday life that the market potential of teenagers and the large screens necessary to capture their interest were unlocked.

Every feature that took off with younger American users had existed before 2010. Cameras have been on phones since 2000, and they sold well. Phones that streamed live broadcasts were already available in 2004 when I was living in Japan. It was not some impressive technical advancement that shifted the market. The growing ubiquity of cellphones in daily life had primed a new, more lucrative market to force the design of cellphones to do a complete 180.

The history of technology is filled with about-faces like this. A certain approach or technique becomes popular but doesn't fit everyone's use case. Companies start experimenting and applying that hot new approach to more and more things until the number of situations where that approach does not work or is not ideal grows into a force that reverses momentum. The industry rediscovers a different way of doing things and swings back.

Engineers praised the publish/subscribe model of Kafka as superior to the hub-and-spoke model of Enterprise Service Buses (ESBs). ESBs

---

7. Robert Triggs, "A Little History of the Smartphone Camera," Android Authority, June 16, 2017, *https://www.androidauthority.com/little-history-smartphone-camera-776711/*.

were a single point of failure and an anti-pattern for service-oriented architecture. Then Kafka added its Connect framework (version 0.9) and its Streams API (0.10), which reintroduced many of the core concepts of ESBs. Google developed Accelerated Mobile Pages to advance asynchronous loading through JavaScript and then added server-side rendering to them—breaking its own spec to move back to a pattern already established by HTML.

Market shifts are complex events. We can see the pattern of technology cycling through the same approaches and structures over and over, but these shifts are less about the superiority of a given characteristic and more about how potential consumers organize themselves.

The User as the Market Co-Creator

Broadly, these kinds of complex compounding shifts are referred to as *Service Dominate Logic (S-D Logic)*. S-D Logic says that consumer value is not created by companies producing products but by an active collaboration between many actors. According to S-D Logic, consumers are not passive, thoughtless sheep whose wants and desires are engineered for them by industry. Instead, consumers actively participate in creating the markets that are leveraged to sell them things.

Consumers and companies create value largely by playing off one another. Anyone who has ever tried to start their own business will tell you the existence of a problem does not mean there's a market for solving it. In 2004, the inability to stream TV and movies from a handheld device easily was not a problem consumers had much interest in having solved. The technology to do so existed by then, but no one was willing to invest hard-earned dollars in a solution to a problem that everyone else had to deal with too. Once cellphones solved the practical problem of keeping in touch with the office when on the move, they appeared in the field of vision of huge numbers of other consumers. This caused other needs to begin to consolidate into marketable problems. You are unlikely to put much thought into the problem of not being able to watch the newest episode of your favorite TV show while flying across the country. But, if you know that other people have such an option and you are missing out, the solution suddenly becomes much more marketable.

The Mainframe and the Cloud

Sometimes, however, the centrifugal forces that govern progress are a lot more basic and fundamental. Let's go back to my story at the beginning of this chapter: Why did we migrate from time-sharing on mainframes to bulky applications on personal computers to time-sharing on the commercial cloud? We could have, for example, continued to develop mainframes until they became clouds. Why didn't we? Why did we spend millions of dollars migrating thousands of applications to a new paradigm only to have to migrate them all back to thinner clients a decade or two later?

Technology is, and probably always will be, an expensive element of any organization's operational model. A great deal of advancement and market co-creation in technology can be understood as the interplay between hardware costs and network costs. Computers are data processors. They move data around and rearrange it into different formats and displays for us. That's about all they do, regardless of whether we use them to play video games or crunch spreadsheets.

All advancements with data processors come down to one of two things: either you make the machine faster or you make the pipes delivering data to the machine faster. These forces cannot grow independently of each other. If the pipes pumping data in get too far ahead of the chips processing data, the machine crashes. If the machine gets too far ahead of the network, the user experiences no actual value add from the increases in speed.

When it becomes possible to create alignable differences by unlocking available improvements in either network speeds or hardware speeds, the whole industry tends to change paradigms to optimize for that improvement. In doing so, it creates a market for the next shift by leaving some potential customers and use cases behind.

Mainframes in their heyday existed in a world where processor power was limited. Having enough of it to make offloading calculations to a machine required investing in a whole room full of equipment and specialized operators, which were expensive. The market invested heavily in making the hardware faster. The lowest-hanging fruit in that endeavor was actually just making the chips smaller so you could pack more of them into the same machine. Doing this did not immediately result in smaller mainframes, but rather it expanded the market to capture different price points so that large organizations would still pay millions of dollars, while small organizations could be persuaded to pay tens of thousands to have mainframes of their own. This exposed computers to a larger audience and stimulated the market for what eventually became the PC. Even still, there wasn't any need to make improvements to network speeds, because the computers were slow and couldn't store much data. A supercomputer in 1985, for example, had about as much processing power as an early-generation iPhone. A more typical computer from that era might have a few hundred kilobytes of RAM and storage. The National Science Foundation Network, which would eventually become the backbone of the early internet, offered 56kbps in the 1980s. At that speed, it would have taken only about an hour to transfer an entire computer's worth of data across the network.

Eventually, decades of engineering work changed that relationship. Faster, more powerful computers were now waiting for their data to come across the network. More and more of these machines were smaller and cheaper with endlessly growing storage capacity. As the number of machines increased, the load on their networks also increased. The more computers connected to a network at the same time, the slower the network becomes. It was going to take time for the demands for more speed to produce a market response, so the industry optimized by shifting toward applications that stored more data locally on the machine itself. We walked away from applications that run on a centralized computer that we communicated with across a network. If we don't need to move data across the network, network speed doesn't hold us back.

The Flat-Rate Internet

At this point, we don't have a cycle; we have a transition. The industry preferences shifted from processing on big centralized machines to smaller, cheaper, local workstations. It's not a spoiler to say that it shifted back because the internet got faster and cheaper, but was that inevitable?

It's unlikely that the private sector ever would have built the internet once it had unlocked the personal computing market. Computer manufacturers were benefiting much more financially from their proprietary standards at the time. The core innovation of the internet was the networking of many different types of networks into one inter-network (hence the name *internet*), which required common standards open to all manufacturers. Building a network that would scale to cross a single country was itself a significant engineering challenge. In fact, many national computer network projects were attempted during the same period as the internet. The United Kingdom had one; France had two; the Soviet Union had three failed attempts. The United States ultimately prevailed because it was not trying to build a national network; it was simply trying to solve compatibility issues caused by all the proprietary standards computer manufacturers were pushing. The US military had funded a number of expensive computers, and it wanted research institutions hundreds of miles away from one another to be able to share those resources. Had it been left up to the computer manufacturers, they obviously would have preferred that all the research institutions bought their own machines.

Nevertheless, the internet was built. Slow and cumbersome at first, without a specific business implementation, it filled up with scholars, hobbyists, futurists, and weirdos. Whereas saturation of the business market unlocked consumers' desire for cellphones as personal entertainment devices, and saturation of the mainframe computer market got smaller organizations with fewer resources looking for smaller machines, the internet penetrated the business market through a slightly anarchist creative community. In 2000, 76 percent of online users were connecting from homes, while 41 percent were connecting from businesses. By 2014, home internet use had exploded to 90 percent, and work internet use remained stagnant at 44 percent.[8]

What's interesting about the internet is that it is the only modern-day communication medium that has been historically flat-rate priced.[9] All packets on the internet are billed basically the same way, regardless of what they are or where they are going.[10] By contrast, you pay more when you call long-distance versus placing a local call, or you pay more when connecting to a cell network in a foreign country versus your own. On the internet, consumers pay more to get faster speeds. That put the pressure on telecommunication companies to compete by making connections faster. The faster the internet became, the more people put on it. The more content that was on the internet, the more consumers started logging on. The more people trying to access a given resource on the internet, the more expensive hosting those resources on your own machines became. Eventually, this flipped the value proposition of the computer industry by making it cheaper to process data "in the cloud" than it was to process it locally. We returned to the notion of

---

8. Susannah Fox and Lee Rainie, "The Web at 25 in the U.S.," Pew Research Center's Internet & American Life Project, February 27, 2014, *https://www.pewresearch.org/internet/2014/02/27/the-web-at-25-in-the-u-s/*.

9. Andrew Odlyzko, "Internet Pricing and the History of Communications," *Computer Networks* 36, 493–517, 2001.

10. You may have heard of "net neutrality," which is the campaign to maintain the flat-rate status of the internet. Initially internet service providers provided a flat rate because it was difficult to charge based on packet type, but alas modern technology makes that more viable.

---

renting time on expensive computers someone else owns versus assuming the costs of buying, maintaining, and upgrading those expensive computers ourselves.

One can track how architectural paradigms fall in and out of favor roughly by whether processing power and storage capacity are growing faster than network speeds; however, faster processors are often a component of what telecoms use to boost their network speeds. This kind of interdependency is true for basically any market. Product development shifts consumer behavior, which shifts product development. Technology doesn't advance in a straight line, because a straight line is not actually efficient. The economy is not a flat plane, but a rich topography with ridges and valleys to navigate around.

The factors that influence shifts are also fractal and interdisciplinary in nature. The reason American internet service providers (ISPs) settled on a flat-rate pricing structure early on is that the landscape offered them two options for building the network of communication lines necessary to be in business in the first place: either they built their own links or they rented other people's links. In the latter category, a wide variety of options were available, not just existing telecom networks built for the telephone, like AT&T, but also private lines maintained by large institutions to connect their data centers. A company like AOL in the 1990s was both in competition with telecoms to sell internet access and a customer of those same telecoms. This made ISPs much more sensitive to customer feedback and the psychological draw of simple, flat pricing a necessity.[11] Among other things, charging for usage levels means services grow more expensive as they get worse. More activity by more users ultimately leads to congestion and degrades network performance. The fact that users have trouble correctly estimating their usage levels and that the majority of them pay more with flat prices further incentivized the

---

[11.] Andrew Odlyzko, "Internet Pricing and the History of Communications," *Computer Networks* 36, 493–517, 2001.

industry. If you want a quick demonstration of that, look up your real cellular data usage and compare it to what limits you are paying for monthly. Most users never come close to exhausting it.

In Europe, it was far more common for telecoms to be government-run, which meant less competition forcing simpler pricing models. The European Union would eventually liberalize the internet market in the late 1990s, while the United States allowed broadband to consolidate. As a result, a lot more competition in Europe has subsequently pushed speeds up and prices down. Today, the internet is faster in many places than it is in the United States. What this means for future shifts in the tech industry is unclear. Any number of factors can change which paradigms are being pushed as best practices. Exposure to technology can create a new market, and that market could run parallel as mainframes and PCs still do, or it could completely overtake another market, just as entertainment-optimized cellphones wiped out BlackBerries and other business-focused phones. Prices could drop. Resources could become scarce. Rarely if ever are these changes fueled by pure technical superiority.

Migrating for Value, Not for Trends

What does any of this have to do with legacy modernization? When people assume that technology advances in a linear fashion, they also assume that anything new is naturally more advanced and better than whatever they are currently running. Adopting new practices doesn't necessarily make technology better, but doing so almost always makes technology more complicated, and more complicated technology is hard to maintain and ultimately more prone to failure.

And yet, information technology that never changes is doomed. It's important to understand that we advance in cycles, because that's the only way we learn how to avoid unnecessary rewrites and partial migrations. Changing technology should be about real value and trade-offs, not faulty assumptions that newer is by default more advanced.

Sometimes it is difficult to compare your use case to the use cases of other seemingly similar organizations. The biggest offender on this front is the commercial cloud, precisely because it adds value to such a broad set of use cases. People tend to assume that means it is a superior technology for all use cases, which is not true. I have a friend who runs a Hadoop cluster to process financial data for the Department of Treasury. Her chief information officer (CIO) insists that they need to shut down the servers they maintain to move this process to the cloud. What the CIO doesn't appreciate is that moving data, while cheaper and easier than it was in the 1980s, is still expensive. There's no question that speed and performance are better if you're processing data in the same place that you're storing it—in this case, on site. Whether Big Data as a Service saves you any money depends on how big your big data actually is, where it is centralized, and how long it takes it to get that big in the first place. Having petabytes of data collected over a five-year period is a different situation from having petabytes generated over the course of a few hours.

Value propositions are often complicated questions for this reason. It's hard enough for a purely technical organization to get it right; it's even harder at organizations where the only people with enough knowledge to advise on these issues are vendors.

CANNIBAL CODE

I f technology advances in cycles, you might assume the best legacy modernization strategy is to wait a decade or two for paradigms to shift back and leapfrog over. If only! For all that mainframes and clouds might have in common in general, they have a number of significant differences in the implementation that block easy transitions. While the architectural philosophy of time-sharing has come back in vogue, other components of technology have been advancing at a different pace. You can divide any single product into an infinite number of elements: hardware, software, interfaces, protocols, and so on. Then you can add specific techniques within those categories. Not all cycles are in sync. The odds of a modern piece of technology perfectly reflecting an older piece of technology are as likely as finding two days where every star in the sky had the exact same position.

So, the takeaway from understanding that technology advances in cycles isn't that upgrades are easier the longer you wait, it's that you should avoid upgrading to new technology simply because it's new.

Alignable Differences and User Interfaces

Without alignable differences, consumers can't determine the value of the technology in which they are being asked to invest. Completely innovative technology is not a viable solution, because it has no reference point to help it find its market. We often think of technology as being streamlined and efficient with no unnecessary bits without a clear purpose, but in fact, many forms of technology you depend on have vestigial features either inherited from other older forms of technology or imported later to create the illusion of feature parity.

For example, most software engineering teams maintain 80-column widths for lines of code. It is easier to read short lines of code than long lines of code; that much is true. But why specifically 80 columns? Why not 100 columns?

Amazingly, an 80-column width is the size of the old mainframe punch cards that were used to input both data and programs into the room-sized computers built during the 1950s and 1960s. So right now, solidly in the 21st century, programmers are enforcing a standard developed for machines most of them have never even seen, let alone programmed.

But, why are mainframe punch cards 80 columns wide? Punch cards used by the forebears of the earliest computer companies—back when they were mechanical "tabulating machines" used primarily for things like the census—were ad hoc and incredibly inefficient. They were designed to tally, not calculate, so they were modeled after what a railroad conductor might use for tickets, rather than for storing data.[1] The cards needed to be fed into machines in batches and then sorted and stored. To avoid having to re-invent everything, the cards themselves were designed to be approximately the same size as the paper currency of the United States at the time: 3¼ by 7⅜ inches. This meant companies could repurpose existing drawers, bins, and boxes to acquire necessary accessories.

---

[1] Geoffrey D. Austrian, *Herman Hollerith: Forgotten Giant of Information Processing* (New York: Columbia University Press, 1982), 124.

By the 1920s, customers were leaning on IBM to get more data storage out of a single card. IBM's innovation was to change the shape of the holes themselves, making them more rectangular so that they could be placed closer together on the card.[2] That meant 80 columns of possible holes.

Now, let's go even deeper. What about the punch card itself? Why were the first computers designed to take input from stiff cards with holes punched into them? Keyboards have existed as long as typewriters, and the first modern typewriter was patented by Christopher Latham Sholes, Carlos Glidden, and Samuel W. Soulé in 1868, nearly a century before some of these mainframes were developed. Telegraphs were experimenting with different types of keyboards even earlier than that. Why would people prefer to punch holes in a thick piece of stock paper when they could just type their information on a keyboard?

The problem with keyboards, or similar input devices, is that it's easy for human operators to mistype things, especially if those human operators get no visual confirmation that what they think they typed is actually what the machine received. Think about typing a password into a field on a website that hides what you type. One disadvantage to such password-masking fields is if you hit the wrong key, you might not notice until the system rejects your input. How many times have you mistyped a password like this? Now imagine inputting an entire message without being able to see what you typed. Operator error was a big concern for telegraphs, especially when they started to play a larger role in ferrying critical messages around the globe.

The solution was to have a keyboard, but instead of interfacing directly with the telegraph, the keyboard would produce a record that could be checked for errors before the machine tried to send the message. Many different variations on this concept were developed, and the one that eventually stuck was punching holes in paper tape.

---

[2] US Patent 1,772,492, Record Sheet for Tabulating Machines, C. D. Lake, filed June 20, 1928, *http://ibm-1401.info/Patent1772492.pdf*.

What's curious about the era of tabulating machines in the late 19th century and the era of early computers in the 20th is that they arrived at the same solution in different ways. The punch cards of tabulating machines were developed from railroad tickets, but the punch cards of telegraphs were developed from the textile industry.

More than a century earlier, French weavers had been automating the pattern designs of elaborate rugs by printing out a design in the form of a series of punched holes on cards and feeding those cards into their looms. This allowed weavers to produce high-quality products much faster, with more artistry and greater accuracy.

The telegraph further refined the system by introducing the concept of encoding. When the goal is to manipulate the threads in a giant loom to create a complex pattern row by row, there's no point in over-complicating things. One hole per raised thread is perfectly effective.

However, when the goal is to send messages long distances, that kind of literalism is inefficient. Telegraph operators were already accustomed to using code to represent different letters, but those codes were optimized to reduce operator error. In Morse code, for example, the most common letters have shorter codes. This keeps transmission fast and minimizes the strain on the operator. Once telegraphs started producing a physical record that the operator could double- or triple-check before sending the message, the most significant gains in performance were to be had by optimizing the encoding for the machines themselves. Letters that were expressed in code length anywhere between one to five units were not easy for machines to deal with. Machines do far better when every letter is equal in length. The best codes now were ones that were a bit more complex, had a fixed length, and ultimately stored more data.

A few different systems were developed. The first one to stick was developed by Emile Baudot in 1870. The so-called Baudot code, aka International Telegraph Alphabet No. 1, was a 5-bit binary system.

Fast-forward to the early computer age when people were developing massive room-sized machines that also were using binary systems.

They needed a way to input data and instructions, but they had no visual interface. Computers wouldn't be developed to work with monitors until 1964 when Bell Labs incorporated the first primitive visual interface into the Multics time-sharing system. We had no way of seeing the input the computer was receiving, so we borrowed an interface from the telegraph, which, in turn, was borrowing one from 18th-century French weavers.

Technology is like that. It progresses in cycles, but those cycles occasionally collide, intersect, or conflate. We are constantly borrowing ideas we've seen elsewhere either to improve our systems or to give our users a reference point that will make adopting the new technology quicker and easier for them. Truly new systems often cannibalize the interfaces of older systems to create alignable differences.

This is why maintaining technology long term is so difficult. Although blindly jumping onto new things for the sake of their newness is dangerous, not keeping up to date is also dangerous. As technology advances, it collects more and more interfaces and patterns. It absorbs them from other fields, and it holds on to historic elements that no longer make sense. It builds assumptions around the most deeply buried characteristics. Keep your systems the way they are for too long, and you get caught trying to migrate decades of assumptions.

Unix Eats the World

A common piece of advice for building successful software is to keep what you are trying to do simple. But what exactly makes one design feel simple and another design feel complicated? Why is a line of code 80 characters long simpler and easier to read? It is short, but what if I told you that user experience research actually puts the ideal number at 50 to 60 characters wide? This means 80 characters is a good 50 percent longer than what we know works best from actual testing.

The human machine is strongly biased toward the familiar. We perceive concepts and constructs we know as simpler, easier, and more efficient just because they are known and comfortable to us. We don't need to be experts in a construct or even necessarily like it in order for familiarity to change our perception of it. In the 1960s, psychologist Robert Zajonc conducted a series of experiments documenting how even a single exposure to something increased positive feelings about it in later encounters. He found this effect with languages, individual words, and images. Later researchers have observed similar preferences in how financial professionals invest,[3] how academic researchers evaluate journals,[4] and what flavors we enjoy when we eat.[5] In psychology, the term for this is the *mere-exposure effect*. Simply being exposed to a concept makes it easier for the brain to process that concept and, therefore, feels easier to understand for the user.

Developing new technology or revitalizing an old system is, therefore, most likely to be effective when building on familiar concepts. Reference points create alignable differences that help us assess the value of something new, but those same reference points make the new technology feel simple and easy, lowering the barrier to entry and increasing the odds it will be adopted as well as the speed of adoption.

Consider the Linux operating system. It's easily one of the most popular operating systems for web servers if not computers in general. Hundreds of variants currently exist that are available to install freely, and there are any number of professional versions. Linux was the uncontested victor to emerge from a mad race to develop an operating system that was both portable to many different types of computers and free of restrictive licenses.

---

3. Gur Huberman, "Familiarity Breeds Investment," *The Review of Financial Studies* 14, no. 3 (June 2001): 659–680, *https://doi.org/10.1093/rfs/14.3.659*.

4. A. Serenko and N. Bontis, "What's Familiar Is Excellent: The Impact of Exposure Effect on Perceived Journal Quality," *J. Informetrics* 5, no. 1 (January 2011): 219–223.

5. Patricia Pliner, "The Effects of Mere Exposure on Liking for Edible Substances," *Appetite* 3, no. 3 (September 1982): 283–290.

Linux is often described as the most popular version of the Unix operating system, except the two OSes share very little when it comes to implementation.

The story of Linux kicks off with the breakup of Bell Systems in 1982, nearly a decade before its creation. A 1956 consent decree against AT&T had forbidden the telecom giant from "any business other than the furnishing of common carrier communications services." This meant that when Bell Labs computer scientists Dennis Ritchie, Ken Thompson, and Rudd Canaday began developing Unix in the 1970s, no one was sure whether AT&T was allowed to sell it. The lawyers at AT&T decided to play it safe and allow it to be sold to academic and research institutions with a copy of its source code along with the software.[6]

Having the source code made it easy to port Unix to different machines as well as modify and debug it. People printed it out and annotated it with their own commentary. Unix became an easy option for teaching students how operating systems worked. It spread like wildfire across a wide variety of different institutions, including universities, museums, governmental organizations, and at least one all-girls private school in the early days.

Users began putting their modified versions of Unix on magnetic tape and making copies to distribute among each other. These essentially were forks and pull requests long before the infrastructure for such things existed. The principal motivation for sharing was to distribute bug fixes and patches.

Meanwhile, AT&T's lawyers were trying to figure out what to do with Unix, and they were waffling between their original determination and a more traditional restrictive approach to intellectual property. Unix historian Peter Salus tells the story of how AT&T's developers actively participated in the piracy of their own intellectual property.

[6.] Peter H. Salus, *The Daemon, the Gnu, and the Penguin* (Keller, TX: Reed Media Services, September 2008).

A large number of bug fixes was collected, and rather than issue them one at a time, a collection tape was put together by Ken [Thompson]. Some of the fixes were quite important. . . . I suspect that a significant number of the fixes were actually done by non-Bell people. Ken tried to send it out, but the lawyers kept stalling and stalling and stalling.

Finally, in complete disgust, someone "found" a tape on Mountain Avenue [the address of Bell Laboratories was 600 Mountain Avenue, Murray Hill, NJ] which had the fixes.

When the lawyers found out about it, they called every licensee and threatened them with dire consequences if they didn't destroy the tape... after trying to find out how they got the tape. I would guess that no one would actually tell them how they came by the tape (I didn't). It was the first of many attempts by the AT&T lawyers to justify their existence and to kill UNIX.[7]

When the university students who studied Unix as part of their computer science degrees graduated and got jobs, they brought Unix with them. AT&T's licensing became more restrictive with every new version, as the company tried to figure out what it legally could do to leverage this thriving community it had accidentally created.

Then in 1982, the US Department of Justice settled its second antitrust case against the telecom and broke up "Ma Bell." AT&T was suddenly free from the consent decree that kept it from treating Unix fully as a product, and it wasted no time in cracking down hard on the community that had grown over the course of a decade.

If you lived through similar attempts to stop sharing other forms of intellectual property, like music and movies, you can understand how once people became accustomed to having Unix as a free and modifiable operating system, they didn't want to give it up and go back to the way things were before. Taking away access to Unix's source code sent the

---

[7] Ibid.

community on the hunt for a replacement that was open sourced and ideally free.

An early contender was a variant of Unix developed at Berkeley called Berkeley Software Distribution (BSD). BSD had a growing community, but it had used part of Unix's source code as its base, so it was quickly bogged down in litigation. The heir to Unix needed to present itself as Unix-like while not including any intellectual property from AT&T.

Enter Linux, which was developed as a pet project by computer science student Linus Torvalds. There was never any intention to create a full operating system from Linux; it was intended to be only a kernel for the specific chip architecture to which the creator happened to have access. The Linux operating system, therefore, was pieced together from a variety of software from other groups. Most of its Unix-like interfaces came from Richard Stallman's GNU project, and GNU itself contained no Unix code by design.

So in a way, Linux is a descendant of Unix that involves no code directly from Unix. But, why hold on to the Unix look and feel at all? Once the decision to start writing something completely new was made, what was the value of wrapping things up to look like Unix? For Stallman, the situation was clear: free software was a moral mission. The goal was not to build a free alternative to Unix, but to build a free *replacement* for Unix that would completely overtake and drive Unix out of business. He did not hesitate to describe the strategy of the GNU project in extremes:

> As the GNU Project's reputation grew, people began offering to donate machines running Unix to the project. These were very useful, because the easiest way to develop components of GNU was to do it on a Unix system, and replace the components of that system one by one. But they raised an ethical issue: whether it was right for us to have a copy of Unix at all.
>
> Unix was (and is) proprietary software, and the GNU Project's philosophy said that we should not use proprietary software. But, applying the same reasoning that leads to the conclusion that violence in self

defense is justified, I concluded that it was legitimate to use a propri-
etary package when that was crucial for developing a free replacement
that would help others stop using the proprietary package.

But, even if this was a justifiable evil, it was still an evil. Today we no
longer have any copies of Unix, because we have replaced them with
free operating systems. If we could not replace a machine's operating
system with a free one, we replaced the machine instead.[8]

Stallman used Unix's interfaces because he understood that if GNU's interfaces matched those of established pieces of software, the users of the proprietary pieces of software would have a bigger incentive to switch.[9]

Let's go down one more level: Why did Unix have the interface it had in the first place? Most Unix commands are two-letter abbreviations for words that don't seem to need abbreviating. The authors of *The UNIX-HATERS Handbook* attribute this interface to the hardware available to Unix's creators:

The novice Unix user is always surprised by Unix's choice of command
names. No amount of training on DOS or the Mac prepares one for the
majestic beauty of cryptic two-letter command names such as cp, rm,
and ls.

Those of us who used early 70s I/O devices suspect the degeneracy stems
from the speed, reliability, and, most importantly, the keyboard of the
ASR-33 Teletype, the common input/output device in those days. Unlike
today's keyboards, where the distance keys travel is based on feedback
principles, and the only force necessary is that needed to close a micro-
switch, keys on the Teletype (at least in memory) needed to travel over

---

8. Chris DiBona, Sam Ockman, and Mark Stone, eds., *Open Sources: Voices from the Open Source Revolution* (Sebastopol, CA: O'Reilly Media, 1999).

9. Ibid.

half an inch, and take the force necessary to run a small electric generator such as those found on bicycles. You could break your knuckles touch typing on those beasts.

If Dennis and Ken had a Selectric instead of a Teletype, we'd probably be typing "copy" and "remove" instead of "cp" and "rm." Proof again that technology limits our choices as often as it expands them.

After more than two decades, what is the excuse for continuing this tradition? The implacable force of history, AKA existing code and books. If a vendor replaced rm by, say, remove, then every book describing Unix would no longer apply to its system, and every shell script that calls rm would also no longer apply. Such a vendor might as well stop implementing the POSIX standard while it was at it.

A century ago, fast typists were jamming their keyboards, so engineers designed the QWERTY keyboard to slow them down. Computer keyboards don't jam, but we're still living with QWERTY today. A century from now, the world will still be living with rm.[10]

Just as programmers are now writing lines of code that would fit on a punch card, they also use operating systems whose interfaces were designed to best fit teletype keyboards. Leveraging familiar constructs to boost adoption can create strange traditions.

Inheritance Paths

If people will more quickly adopt technology that follows an already familiar pattern, even one they hate, it's worth exploring how people become exposed to certain patterns in the first place. From the very beginning, computing has been a cross-functional industry. Networks of people are formed around the development of computers and the

---

[10] Simson Garfinkel, Daniel Weise, and Steven Strassmann, eds., *The UNIX-HATERS Handbook* (San Mateo, CA: IDG Books, 1994), 18–19.

professions most likely to use computers to do other work. In the early days of computers, this meant computer users were both the computer scientists who built applications, developed languages, and designed architectures *and* the professionals such as scientists, mathematicians, and bankers. Even today, these groups have a tendency to silo themselves, limiting their exposure to interfaces created for other use cases.

Consider the following: one of the most successful early programming languages is COBOL, and yet modern programming languages have inherited very little of COBOL's design patterns. For example, we do not section code off into divisions, nor do we use periods to end lines of code. Few programmers would guess that PIC is a variable character string. Some of COBOL's features have reappeared in other languages, but very little of its syntax and interface was retained. Instead, COBOL itself has adopted many constructs from later languages in an effort to clean up its act.

On the other hand, ALGOL60 has profoundly shaped the structure and syntax of virtually every modern language, but you'd struggle to find a programmer today who has ever even heard of it.[11]

When we examine the accomplishments of various programming languages, COBOL is the obvious winner. COBOL programs still shuffle millions of transactions and trillions of dollars from point A to point B. It's hard to name a single thing of significance that was ever implemented in ALGOL60. The language BCPL, a similarly influential and obscure descendent of ALGOL60, survived just long enough to become the grandfather of C. So how on Earth did the patterns of failed languages become more familiar to early computer scientists than the patterns of the first truly successful, cross-platform high-level programming language?

The answer is that COBOL was a language built for people who did not want to understand how the computer worked; they just wanted

---

[11] History buffs and recovering anthropologists do not count.

to get the job done. When the Committee on Data Systems Languages (CODASYL) was developing COBOL, the attitude among those devoted to the study and development of computers was that you should learn the flavor of Assembly relevant for your particular machine. Making programming more accessible and code human-readable was considered an anti-pattern, dumbing down the beauty of programming for an unworthy audience.

This audience, however, was made up of people who actually used computers for practical purposes, and many of them were largely unamused by the idea that they should rewrite their programs every single time they upgraded their machines. This group of people didn't care about being "real programmers." They cared about getting stuff done, better and faster than the competition if possible. Technical correctness didn't matter. Elegance didn't matter. Execution mattered, and anything that lowered the barrier to using computers to execute their goals was preferable to more powerful tools that were harder to learn.

Computer scientists during this period had opposite incentives. While COBOL users were judged and rewarded based on their ability to get nontechnical things done faster with computers, ALGOL60 users were judged and rewarded based on their ability to expand the functionality of what was even possible to do with the machines in the first place. Typically, there were two types of accomplishments in this space: get the machine to do something new or get the machine to do something more efficiently than before. For computer scientists, the programming language *was* the output. After it was developed, the next step was not to write programs, but to write papers about the language and share them with other academics for feedback and study.

Roughly three networks of people were programming computers between the 1950s and 1970s: scientists and mathematicians, data processors, and academics or computer researchers.

Scientists and mathematicians used computers for calculations, and they preferred languages that reflected scientific and mathematical notation as much as possible. This community popularized FORTRAN.[12] When two math professors at Dartmouth wanted to create a language to make programming more accessible to students, they borrowed heavily from the syntax of FORTRAN II to develop BASIC. BASIC went on to spawn hundreds of variants, many of which are still in use today.

Data processors used computers to read data from one source and either run calculations or transform that data in some way before saving it to another source. These were the COBOL users, and that language proved so effective, it is still being used today.

If you want proof that adoption is influenced by shared knowledge among networks of people and not strictly merit, consider this: the organizations that are trying to replace their old COBOL applications today are not migrating them to what would be the first choice for data processing among modern programming languages, which is Python, but to the language that has inherited COBOL's market of a common language for businesses, which is Java.

The design of the language is never what's important; it's the people. The type of people who would have become COBOL programmers before are now becoming Java programmers, making Java the natural choice, despite that it was not designed to handle the use case for which COBOL was optimized.

Perhaps that's why so much COBOL remains in place, having resisted all attempts to eliminate it.

Academics and computer researchers focused on the development of computers. When they finally moved off Assembly, it was onto languages specifically for documenting and implementing algorithms. ALGOL60 may not have been used to build many applications, but it was what the Association for Computing Machinery (ACM) used to describe

---

12. FORTRAN is itself an abbreviation of Formula Translation.

algorithms in textbooks and academic sources for more than 30 years. This made it a powerful influence on the languages researchers later developed.

The University of Cambridge developed the Cambridge Programming Language (CPL) based on ALGOL60. CPL led to BCPL, which was stripped down to create B, which was further modified to create C. Next, C became the programming language of choice for this group of users, and it led to the development of a huge number of languages used by all kinds of programmers: Java, Go, PHP (via Perl), Ruby, Python, and Swift.

Also popular with this group were the Lisps. Because the original Lisp was only a theoretical design document, to this day, waves of different implementations spring up quickly followed by futile attempts to standardize. During the 1960s and 1970s, Lisp was strongly associated with AI research and largely was relegated to that niche. Ironically, our own era of computing has seen much more progress in AI, but Lisp hardly plays a critical role. Instead, today's Lisps are seen as a family of general programming languages that occasionally inject ideas and structures into more mainstream languages.

So this pivotal moment of computer science history had two groups of people who programmed in order to achieve some practical purpose not related to the computers themselves and one group that worked with computers to push the boundaries of what the computers themselves could do. The bulk of languages that exist retain the constructs that were familiar to this third group of programmers, even though COBOL, FORTRAN, and BASIC had a much wider community of users.

Overall, interfaces and ideas spread through networks of people, not based on merit or success. Exposure to a given configuration creates the perception that it's easier and more intuitive, causing it to be passed down to more generations of technology. The lesson to learn here is the systems that feel familiar to people always provide more value than the systems that have structural elegances but run contrary to expectations.

Leveraging Interfaces When Approaching Legacy Systems

When I'm working on a legacy system, I always start off by evaluating the prospective users. Who will be maintaining this system long term? What technologies are they comfortable with? Who will be using this system the most? How do they expect the system to work?

That doesn't mean things can't be changed or new concepts can't be introduced. Particularly if the system is a couple decades old, the interfaces are probably tied to processes and associations that don't make sense anymore, just like the way 80-character lines come from punch cards, two-character Linux commands come from teletype machines, and the save icon on desktop applications is a floppy disk. Sometimes changing interfaces to get rid of requirements that are no longer relevant is a good thing. Defining what the requirements of a minimum viable product (MVP) would be today if the system were brand new is a great thought experiment to run when formalizing a plan of attack.

However, even when the result of change is net positive, changing interfaces is not free. Making people think adds friction and increases the odds of failure, even if the new interface is better and more consistent with the overall vision of the product.

Engineers tend to overestimate the value of order and neatness. The only thing that really matters with a computer system is its effectiveness at performing its practical application. Linux did not come to dominate the operating system world because it had been artfully designed from scratch; it scraped together ideas and implementations from a number of different systems and focused on adding value in one key place, the kernel.

The incentives that reward individual software engineers for their uniqueness, their ability to do new things, or to do old things in innovative ways are still present, even if the desire to publish papers in academic journals has been supplanted by the desire to write popular blog posts. Yet technology is more likely to be successful when it builds on common things. These two forces are always in tension with any software project, but legacy systems are particularly vulnerable.

We know, for example, that iterating on existing solutions is more likely to improve software than a full rewrite. The dangers of full rewrites have been documented. Joel Spolsky of Fog Creek Software and Stack Overflow described them as "the single worst strategic mistake that any software company can make."[13] Chad Fowler, general manager of startups at Microsoft, describes it this way:

Almost all production software is in such bad shape that it would be nearly useless as a guide to re-implementing itself. Now take this already bad picture, and extract only those products that are big, complex, and fragile enough to need a major rewrite, and the odds of success with this approach are significantly worse.[14]

Fred Brooks coined the term *second system syndrome* in 1975 to explain the tendency of such full rewrites to produce bloated, inefficient, and often nonfunctioning software. But he attributed such problems not to the rewrites themselves, but to the experience of the architects overseeing the rewrite. The second system in second system syndrome was not the second version of an existing system, it was the second system the architect had produced. Brooks's feeling was that architects are stricter with their first systems because they have never built software before, but for their second systems, they become overconfident and tack on all kinds of flourishes and features that ultimately overcomplicate things. By their third systems, they have learned their lesson.

---

13. Joel Spolsky, "Things You Should Never Do, Part I," Joel on Software, April 6, 2000, *https://www.joelonsoftware.com/2000/04/06/things-you-should-never-do-part-i/*.

14. Chad Fowler, "Software as Spec," December 28, 2006, *http://chadfowler.com/2006/12/28/software-as-spec.html*.

Unfortunately, when confronted with the troubles of existing systems, engineering teams tend to build the most momentum around starting from scratch. Initiatives to repair and restore operational excellence gradually, much the way one would fix up an old house, tend to have few volunteers among engineering teams. That's because Zajonc's mere-exposure effect has an upper bound. There's a point where familiarity breeds contempt.

From an economic perspective, there's a difference between risk and *ambiguity*.[15] Risks are known and estimable threats; ambiguities are places where outcomes both positive and negative are unknown. The traditional school of thought tells us that human beings are averse to ambiguity and will avoid it as much as possible. However, ambiguity aversion is one of those decision-making models that test well in laboratories but break down when brought into the real world where decisions are more complex and probabilities less clearly defined. Specifically when the decision involves multiple attributes, a positive framing of the problem can flip people's behavior from ambiguity-avoiding to ambiguity-seeking.[16]

The incentives of individual praise aside, engineering teams tend to gravitate toward full rewrites because they incorrectly think of old systems as specs. They assume that since an old system works, all technical challenges and possible problems have been settled. The risks have been eliminated! They can add more features to the new system or make changes to the underlying architecture without worry. Either they do not perceive the ambiguity these changes introduce or they see such ambiguity positively, imagining only gains in performance and the potential for greater innovation.

[15.] Frank H. Knight, *Risk, Uncertainty, and Profit* (Boston: Houghton Mifflin Company, 1921).

[16.] Vicki M. Bier and Brad L. Connell, "Ambiguity Seeking in Multi-Attribute Decisions: Effects of Optimism and Message Framing," *Journal of Behavioral Decision Making* 7, no. 3 (September 1994): 169–182, *https://doi.org/10.1002/bdm.3960070303*.

Meanwhile, the existing system has little ambiguity left. It is what it is, hypothetical potential exhausted. We know that past the upper bound of mere exposure, once people find a characteristic they do not like, they tend to judge every characteristic discovered after that more negatively.[17] So programmers prefer full rewrites over iterating legacy systems because rewrites maintain an attractive level of ambiguity while the existing systems are well known and, therefore, boring. It's no accident that proposals for full rewrites tend to include introducing some language, design pattern, or technology that is new to the engineering team. Very few rewrite plans take the form of redesigning the system using the same language or merely fixing a well-defined structural issue. The goal of full rewrites is to restore ambiguity and, therefore, enthusiasm. They fail because the assumption that the old system can be used as a spec and be trusted to have diagnosed accurately and eliminated every risk is wrong.

Beware Artificial Consistency

In the next chapter, I'll go into detail about how to balance these tensions to develop a strategy around when to reinvent and rewrite and when to leverage existing and familiar interfaces. But for now, the takeaway from this exploration of how traits are passed down should be that perception of simplicity is influenced by what your use case for technology exposes you to. Things seem easier when they are familiar. Familiarity is determined by what you are doing with technology and who you are doing it with.

But familiarity has downsides as well. While working with legacy systems, you'll find yourself fielding many proposals that claim to improve the system largely by establishing artificial consistency. *Artificial consistency* means restricting design patterns and solutions to a small pool

---

[17.] Michael Norton and Jean Frost, "Less Is More: The Lure of Ambiguity, or Why Familiarity Breeds Contempt," *Journal of Personality and Social Psychology* 92 (January 2007): 97–105, *https://doi.org/10.1037/0022-3514.92.1.97*.

that can be standardized and repeated throughout the entire architecture in a way that does not provide technical value. What's important to understand about artificial consistency is that it focuses on consistency of form and classification over functionality. As an example, Node.js and React.js are both forms of JavaScript. These two technologies look consistent, but they do different things and are built upon different abstractions. The fact that they are both forms of JavaScript doesn't give Node.js an edge when interacting with React.js over any other backend language that an engineering team might choose instead. An engineer's skill in one does not necessarily translate to the other.

Artificial consistency can bring value to nontechnical processes. For example, standardizing on one programming language makes recruiting, hiring, and, ultimately, sharing engineering resources much easier. But when the principal purpose of a modernization effort is to provide technical value, be careful not to be seduced by the assumption that things that look the same, or that we use the same words to describe, actually integrate better.

Another place where artificial consistency comes into play is with databases. The top choices for databases 10 years ago are not the top choices today, so senior leaders sometimes will ask that legacy databases be migrated to another option more consistent with whatever newer systems are using. As with the previous example, there are legitimate nontechnical reasons to do this, such as not wanting the expense of supporting two different databases that essentially behave the same way, but the issue quickly can get out of hand when the engineering team is being asked to remove the key value store they're using for a cache in favor of a relational database.

Figuring out when consistency adds technical value and when it is artificial is one of the hardest decisions an engineering team must make. Human beings are pattern-matching machines. The flip side of finding familiar things easier is that we tend to over-optimize, giving in to artificial consistency when better tools are available to us.

EVALUATING YOUR ARCHITECTURE

A big red flag is raised for me when people talk about the phases of their modernization plans in terms of which *technologies* they are going to use rather than what *value* they will add. This distinction is usually a pretty clear sign that they assume anything new must be better and more advanced than what they already have.

It may seem picky to focus on language, but communication is an essential part of keeping modernization on track. Teams tend to move in the direction they are looking. If we talk about what we're doing in terms of technical choices, users' needs get lost. The best way to find value is by focusing on their needs.

I always keep in mind three principles when developing a strategy around a new legacy system. The tour of history in Chapters 1 and 2 laid them out in detail:

- Modernizations should be based on adding value, not chasing new technology.

- Familiar interfaces help speed up adoption.

- People gain awareness of interfaces and technology through their networks, not necessarily by popularity.

But for most organizations, the conversation around modernization begins with failure. No one would invest the time and effort if the system were humming along just fine. The term *legacy modernization* itself is a little misleading. Plenty of old systems exist that no one gives a thought to changing because they just work.

So the last thing you need to consider when developing a plan of attack is the exact nature of the failure that is driving the desire to modernize in the first place. In all likelihood, you're dealing with one or more of the following issues: technical debt, poor performance, or instability.

Problem 1: Technical Debt

Old systems don't need to be modernized simply because they are old. Lots of technology has not fundamentally changed in decades. Moving to the latest and greatest thing can sometimes cause more problems than it solves.

The following situations might warrant modernization:

- The code is difficult to understand. It references decisions or architectural choices that are no longer relevant, and institutional memory has been lost.

- Qualified engineering candidates are rare.

- Hardware replacement parts are difficult to find.

- The technology can no longer perform its function efficiently.

The terms *legacy* and *technical debt* are frequently conflated. They are different concepts, although a system can show signs of both problems.

Legacy refers to an old system. Its design patterns are relatively consistent, but they are out-of-date. Upgrading the capacity of the underlying infrastructure results in performance increases. New engineers are difficult to onboard because of the skills gap between the technology they know and the technology with which the legacy system was built.

Technical debt, by contrast, can (and does) happen at any age. It's a product of subpar trade-offs: partial migrations, quick patches, and out-of-date or unnecessary dependencies. Technical debt is most likely to happen when assumptions or requirements have changed and the organization resorts to a quick fix rather than budgeting the time and resources to adapt. Unlike legacy systems, performance issues in this case are usually a byproduct of inefficient code instead of out-of-date infrastructure. Upgrading the infrastructure—increasing memory and cores or adding servers—doesn't always produce equal increases in performance.

Systems with substantial technical debt also make it difficult to onboard new engineers, but in this case, the difficulty is because the application's internal logic doesn't make sense. Perhaps the documentation is out-of-date, or levels of abstraction are piled up on top of one another, or functions are named unintuitively.

Managing technical debt is about restoring consistency. A good way to approach the challenge is to run a product discovery exercise as if you were going to build a completely new system, but don't actually build one! Instead, use this new vision to excavate and refocus the current system.

As time passes, requirements naturally change. As requirements change, usage patterns change, and the organization and design that is most efficient also changes. Use product discovery to redefine what your MVP is, and then find where that MVP is in the existing code. How are these sets of functions and features organized? How would you organize them today?

Another useful exercise to run when dealing with technical debt is to compare the technology available when the system was originally built to the technology we would use for those same requirements today. I employ this technique a lot when dealing with systems written in COBOL. For all that people talk about COBOL dying off, it is good at certain tasks. The problem with most old COBOL systems is that they were designed at a time when COBOL was the *only* option. If the goal is to get rid of COBOL, I start by sorting which parts of the system are in COBOL because COBOL is good at performing that task, and which parts are in COBOL because there were no other tools available. Once we have that mapping, we start by pulling the latter off into separate services that are written and designed using the technology we would choose for that task today.

Example: The General Ledger

One such debt-heavy system was designed as a *general ledger* for a large healthcare organization. It is a complex system involving multiple mainframes working together. It processes requests from still more mainframes that back other systems that need to issue payments. The general ledger's core function is to authorize and issue payments from an organization to third parties. The system, therefore, must make sure the organization has the funds to issue the payment, that the request is valid, that the request is not a duplicate, and that the circumstances of the request comply with all relevant regulations. In addition, this system also tracks money owed to the organization, sends requests to remind debtors to pay, and generates reports for various stakeholders.

The current system organizes code based on division—for example, Loans and Accounts Payable are different applications within the system despite having overlapping requirements—and is written in COBOL or the Assembly language specific to the mainframe that typically runs its jobs. Overall, the system looks something like Figure 3-1.

It's easy to see how this system evolved this way. The organization is large with a lot of money to spend, and when computers were first being introduced to the market, it took advantage of them right away (hence, the Assembly). The organization migrated paper processes to digital processes largely without changing them and maintains the original process boundaries within the technology.

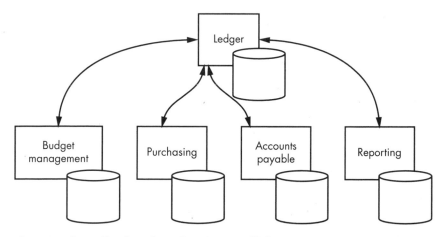

Figure 3-1: *The applications that talk to the general ledger*

Back then, computers were "extras," big experimental toys to make things faster, and not every business unit felt the new machines would add value to their process. The final system ended up divided by business unit because the adoption of technology was gradual, unit by unit.

But today, computers are the default, so this is not the way we would build such a system. We might preserve the mapping of applications to divisions, but we would build shared services that reflected their shared requirements. Some features play to COBOL's strengths of processing large amounts of financial data accurately, but COBOL doesn't necessarily bring much to the table when generating reports or sending out mailings.

In modernizing this system, I would identify the appropriate shared services and then select one to build. The ideal situation is when I can identify an application that needs only one of the proposed shared services. We build that service and rewrite that application to use it. Then we go back and find an application that needs that shared service plus another shared service on our list. We build the second shared service and rewrite the application to use both.

However, rarely can applications in large systems be arranged in order of ascending complexity in that manner. More likely, we will have to pull out one shared service and rewrite each application one by one, before pulling out a second shared service and rewriting each application one by one. This can be frustrating, but it's important not to increase load on a new service before we have enough experience with it to know what normal behavior looks like.

Problem 2: Performance Issues

Performance issues are actually one of the nicer problems to have with legacy systems. Few organizations are motivated to do anything about legacy systems until they start affecting the business side and work starts to slow down. Sometimes this is because the system itself has slowed down, but more likely, the system's performance has remained pretty static and literally everything around it has gotten faster.

Normally, the issues of how long something should take and how many resources it needs to do the job are highly subjective. People tend to accept the current state as fine, especially if they have limited experience with other systems. If the organization believes its system is having performance issues, the hard work of figuring out what "better" is has already been done for you. A system cannot have performance issues unless the organization that owns it has defined expectations.

This book will repeat the message of trade-offs over and over again. No changes made to existing systems are free. Changes that improve one characteristic of a system often make something else harder. Teams that are good at legacy modernization know how to identify the trade-offs and negotiate the best possible deal. You have to pick a goal or a characteristic to optimize on and set budgets for all other characteristics so you know how much you're willing to give up before you start losing value.

Is it worth losing some accuracy to make things faster? Is it worth migrating to managed services when that makes testing locally more difficult? When an organization has decided its system has performance issues, it is easier to answer these questions. The organization must have some expectation of how fast performance should be or how much money it should spend to satisfy requirements.

Once performance requirements are defined, the task of evaluating the legacy system and developing a strategy becomes about listing all the steps in a given task and identifying performance bottlenecks. With that mapped out, you can prioritize improvements, starting with the areas where the most gains can be realized.

Tackling each bottleneck should not require eliminating it completely. If you can do that, great, but in most cases, you'll find that what you would need to invest to eliminate it is not worth the boost in performance. Don't underestimate the power of 5 percent, 10 percent, and 20 percent performance gains. As long as your approach to reaching those gains moves the system toward a better overall state, a 5 percent gain can pay interest as the project moves forward. Other changes may turn that 5 percent into a 30 percent or 50 percent gain later.

That being said, don't throw out engineering best practices and good architecture just to patch something up and get a performance boost. You can spot such solutions because they often avoid touching what is obviously the real problem. The people who propose these solutions are often frustrated by the system's problems and overwhelmed by the possibility of investing months or years in incremental improvement. They argue against the 5 percent change that makes the system better because they believe a 5 percent improvement will never be enough. Instead, they propose a solution that offers a much larger performance gain, but that compounds the root cause or makes it more difficult to fix later. Here's one example of what I mean. We had a system where multiple services needed access to a giant unstructured data store. The data had grown to a size that deleting some of it from the data store was such a resource-intensive process, it affected the performance of normal reads and writes.

The problem was the unstructured nature of the data and the fact that so many services needed to access it at one time, but that is a hard problem to solve. The process of breaking up the data, structuring it appropriately, and migrating services over would take months, if not years. Instead, the engineers on the project wanted to build a garbage collection service that would run deletes during low traffic periods when the performance hit wasn't as big an issue.

What's the problem with this approach? To begin with, creating a new service is no small amount of work, and once created, it has to be maintained, monitored, tested, and scaled. On top of that, the new service is an abstraction to perform a potentially dangerous operation outside the normal flow of events. What triggers this service, and how do we know the job it's running is correct? Adding a new service just increases the overall complexity of the system to take advantage of a temporary situation. As load continues to increase, those low-traffic windows will be smaller and harder to find.

Adding this system, if it worked, could produce a huge gain in performance that would buy the organization time to fix the real problem. Certainly that was the intention of the engineers who were proposing it. But it's also possible that once such a bandage was in place, the organization would lose interest in fixing the real problem, and this team would have accomplished nothing more than resetting the clock on the time bomb.

The smarter thing to do would be to look for the baby steps toward breaking up the data that would have produced those 5 or 10 percent gains. Such gains add up if you find enough of them.

Large problems are always tackled by breaking them down into smaller problems. Solve enough small problems, and eventually the large problem collapses and can be resolved.

Example: Case Flow Management

Software built to manage an application through multistaged approval processes are performance battlegrounds as they age. Here's an example of a system where we could increase its output just by finding enough bottlenecks that could be whittled down. The technology behind this application approval process is reasonably good, but some parts of the process are automated, and some are manual. Some parts are digital, and some are still on paper. Some parts were digitalized recently and some 20 years ago. Everyone agrees that the system would be better if the remaining parts that could be automated were automated, if the paper parts of the process were digitalized, and if the older components of the system were brought up to speed, but that's a long list of improvements.

Not all of the highest priority tasks actually affect the time it takes to process an application. For example, at one point in the process, the applicant must sign a consent form authorizing the organization to run a background check. Although the paper form could be replaced with a simple web form or an integration with a third-party service, this part of the application process is often done in parallel with processing the rest of the application. Therefore, digitalizing that step does not actually speed up the total processing time of a single application.

Other seemingly irrelevant issues could make a much bigger difference. Cases were being sent to the background-check service in batches. If one application within that batch had a problem, all the applications in that batch had to wait for it to be resolved before moving on. Simply reconfiguring jobs into batches of one could save a lot of time.

Instead of looking at the purely technical improvements to the system, the team decreased the processing time for an average application by tracing the application's path. They had already done the hard work of determining a better system meant faster application turnaround, and they structured their approach around optimizing for that.

Problem 3: Stability Issues

On the other hand, some legacy systems perform their core functions within the parameters the organization needs to be successful, but they are unstable. They are not too slow; they produce the correct result and within the resources the organizations has available for the task, but there are frequent "surprises," such as outages with bizarre black-swan-style root causes or routine upgrades that sometimes go very poorly. Ongoing development work is stopped because unforeseen technical conflicts pop up and need to be resolved.

In 1983, Charles Perrow coined the term *normal accidents* to describe systems that were so prone to failure, no amount of safety procedures could eliminate accidents entirely. According to Perrow, normal accidents are not the product of bad technology or incompetent staff. Systems that experience normal accidents display two important characteristics.

They are tightly coupled. When two separate components are dependent on each other, they are said to be coupled. In tightly coupled situations, there's a high probability that changes with one component will affect the other. For example, if a change to one code base requires a corresponding change to another code base, the two repositories are tightly coupled. Loosely coupled components, on the other hand, are ones where changes made to one component don't necessarily affect the other.

Tightly coupled systems produce cascading effects. One change creates a response in another part of the system, which creates a response in another part of the system. Like a domino effect, parts of the system start executing without a human operator telling them to do so. If the system is simple, it is possible to anticipate how failure will happen and prevent it, which leads to the second characteristic of systems that experience normal accidents.

They are complex. Big systems are often complex, but not all complex systems are big. Signs of complexity in software include the number of direct dependencies and the depth of the dependency tree, the number of integrations, the hierarchy of users and ability to delegate, the number of edge cases the system must control for, the amount of input from untrusted sources, the amount of legal variety in that input, and so on, and so forth. Computer systems naturally grow more complex as they age, because as they age, we tend to add more and more features to them, which increases at least a few of these charac-teristics. Computer systems also tend to start off tightly coupled and may in fact stay that way if priority is not given to refactoring the code occasionally.

Tightly coupled and complex systems are prone to failure because the coupling produces cascading effects, and the complexity makes the direction and course of those cascades impossible to predict.

If your goal is to reduce failures or minimize security risks, your best bet is to start by evaluating your system on those two characteristics: Where are things tightly coupled, and where are things complex? Your goal should not be to eliminate all complexity and all coupling; there will be trade-offs in each specific instance.

Suppose you have three services that need to access the same data. If you configure them to talk to the same database, they are tightly coupled (Figure 3-2).

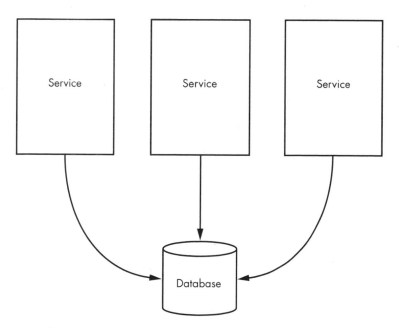

Figure 3-2: *Tightly coupled services*

Such coupling creates a few potential problems. To begin with, any of the three services could make a change to the data that breaks the other two services. Any changes to the database schema have to be coordinated across all three services. By sharing a database, you lose the scaling benefit of having three separate services, because as load increases on one service, it is passed down to the database, and the other services see a dip in performance.

However, giving each service its own database trades those problems for other potential problems. You now must figure out how to keep the data between the three separate databases consistent.

Loosening up the coupling of two components usually ends with the creation of additional abstraction layers, which raises complexity on the system. Minimizing the complexity of systems tends to mean more reuse of common components, which tightens couplings. It's not about transforming your legacy system into something that is completely simple and uncoupled, it's about being strategic as to where you are coupled and where you are complex and to what degree. Places of complexity are areas where the human operators make the most mistakes and have the greatest probability of misunderstanding. Places of tight coupling are areas of acceleration where effects both good and bad will move faster, which means less time for intervention.

Once you have identified the parts of the system where there is tight coupling and where there is complexity, study the role those areas have played in past problems. Will changing the ratio of complexity to coupling make those problems better or worse?

A helpful way to think about this is to classify the types of failures you've seen so far. Problems that are caused by human beings failing to read something, understand something, or check something are usually improved by minimizing complexity. Problems that are caused by failures in monitoring or testing are usually improved by loosening the coupling (and thereby creating places for automated testing). Remember also that an incident can include both elements, so be thoughtful in your analysis. A human operator may have made a mistake to trigger an incident, but if that mistake was impossible to discover because the logs weren't granular enough, minimizing complexity will not pay off as much as changing the coupling.

Example: Custom Configuration

Consider an organization that wanted to increase the power of custom configurations on its monolithic application. It built a configuration service that would allow its software engineers to set flags through the monolith's code (Figure 3-3). The application sends requests to the service with the identity of the user to fetch the appropriate configuration value. Since those values rarely change, more than 90 percent of the requests are handled by a cache. If the cache fails, the request moves on to a simple web service that immediately retries the cache before ultimately going back to the database to retrieve the configuration setting. The database is separate from the monolith's database, but it runs on the same virtual machine (VM). Traffic directly from the application connects with the monolith's database. The custom configuration database uses about 1 percent of the VM resources.

When the service receives the configuration value from the database, it updates the cache and sends the data back to the monolith. The data

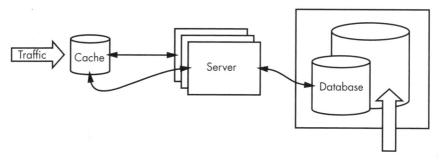

Figure 3-3: Requests moving through the custom configuration service

on custom configurations is stored in a key-value style, with the key being the identity of the user and the value being a dictionary with all relevant configuration settings. Because possible customizations are almost infinite, these dictionaries do not have standard schemas. If a user has no configuration value set for a given flag, it is not present at all in the dictionary. The cache preserves this structure.

In general, this service performs well for the organization, but it has quirks that are difficult for engineers to reproduce and even harder to diagnose. A few problems have been traced back to cache stampedes. Users rarely change values after setting them, but in the rare cases where the cache does need to be updated, the whole dictionary is affected.

How can we think of this part of the system in terms of complexity and coupling? The monolith's behavior is coupled to the configuration service. If the configuration service goes down, the monolith either cannot fulfill requests or falls back to a default value that might completely change the user's experience. If the configuration service experiences partial outages, the monolith's behavior becomes wildly unpredictable.

Hosting the databases on the same VM creates coupling between the monolith and the configuration service. If the monolith's database has performance issues, the configuration service's database feels them, and vice versa. However, in this case, fixing that issue by moving the configuration service's database to its own VM might not bring much value. If the monolith's database is having problems, the product itself is likely down, making the performance of this service largely irrelevant. Since the service uses only 1 percent of the VM's resources, it is unlikely that it will affect the monolith without first triggering pages to the engineer on call. We might want to separate them for the sake of right-scaling, but that increases the number of VMs we're paying for and doesn't necessarily buy us much more than cosmetic improvements on our architectural diagram.

On the complexity side, the data structure was probably a poor design choice. When the monolith makes a request, it does not need every value set for the user, only the value relevant at that moment. If the key in the key-value store was user ID plus flag ID, the data could be flat, which would mitigate the risk of cache stampedes. On the other hand, we could keep the data structured as is and change the monolith's assumptions so that it requests the user's dictionary only once and stores the data returned in memory for the lifetime of the session. That solution minimizes the coupling between the monolith and the service, but it increases complexity. We need to understand how much data we would be storing in memory at any one point, and at what level that becomes problematic. We need to define a time to live and how to implement it. Will we want to make sure all the users' requests are directed to the same server, or should we just assume that if a session is live, all servers in the application cluster will query the configuration service at least once and store the same data in their memory?

Stages of a Modernization Plan

One day during a one-on-one, an engineer on my team confessed to feeling that we had approached our work on one legacy system completely wrong. I had recently brought a new engineer onto the team and given her explicit instructions to tear through the system's testing suites. Although the tests were comprehensive and the coverage was good, they were brittle, poorly organized, and difficult to make sense of. That was a reflection of the system's overall design, so the new engineer set about refactoring huge parts of how the code was organized, making it easier to test and the tests more reliable.

Looking at the new engineer's contributions, my engineer knew this configuration was better. For months, we had been working on this system. She was kicking herself for not looking at the problem the way the newcomer did. "We were too pragmatic," she said. "We just conformed to the system's existing patterns when we should have redone it."

I disagreed. What my engineer had forgotten was that when we took on this system, it was unstable. Things would frequently go wrong silently. Errors weren't properly handled or logged. Performance was an issue.

It was good to learn how to have that kind of technical vision the new engineer displayed. I certainly wasn't going to discourage my team from studying her contributions, but it was right to be pragmatic in the beginning. When you first take on a legacy system, you can't possibly understand it well enough to make big changes right away. As part of those pragmatic changes, we also invested a lot of time documenting and researching the system. Truth be told, the new engineer's first assignment was a series of small, pragmatic changes designed to help her get to know the system too, but by that point, my engineers knew the system so well, they were able to onboard her much quicker. She tore through those assignments in a matter of days.

"How do you think handling a major refactoring at the same time that we were having regular incidents would have affected you?" I asked.

"It would have been really stressful."

So stressful, in fact, that it would have compromised the team's judgment. These are the kinds of situations where people become frustrated and start convincing themselves that the best thing to do is throw the whole thing out and build it from scratch.

When both observability and testing are lacking on your legacy system, observability comes first. Tests tell you only what *won't* fail; monitoring tells you what *is* failing. Our new engineer had the freedom to alter huge swaths of the system because the work the team had done rolling out better monitoring meant when her changes were deployed, we could spot problems quickly.

But the real lesson here is that modernization plans evolve as they progress. The first stage is one of evaluation. This doesn't necessarily mean you should stop everything and produce big complicated plans, but you should focus on low-hanging fruit of immediate issues with pragmatic fixes. Use these small tasks to focus your investigation of the system itself. Get to know it and its quirks. Where are your blind spots in terms of monitoring? How easy is it to change things, test them, and be confident that they will work? Where are the gaps where the official documentation says things work this way, but they don't? How much dead code is there? And so on, and so forth.

When your team knows the system well enough, you can expand the scope to look at issues across the system. Are things organized the way they should be? Is there a better technology to incorporate now, perhaps a different programming language or a new tool?

On particularly large systems, it is a good idea to make this an iterative multilevel process. In other words, pick one part of the large system and focus on that. Look at small pragmatic issues, and then look at more global issues within the component. Take a further step back and look for those global issues elsewhere in the system itself before deciding on an approach to them. Zoom back down to fix the component's global issues and move on to the next component. Continue this local-global-super-global routine until the system is where you need it to be.

The deeper your team understands the system and its quirks, the more predictable the system's behavior is on a day-to-day basis and the easier it is to make big changes.

No Silver Bullets

The only real rule of modernizing legacy systems is that there are no silver bullets. The rest of this chapter outlines different styles of organizing development activities. You will likely use all of them at different points on a large project.

The key thing to remember is that this is a toolkit. You break down large problems into smaller problems, and you choose the tool that gives you the highest probability of success with that specific problem. Sure, you may use some methods more often than others, but every large-scale legacy system has at least one square peg to contend with. It's impossible to finish the job if all you know how to do is solve for round holes.

Full Rewrite

A *full rewrite* is exactly what it sounds like: you start over with the intention of building a totally new system. The trouble with this approach is what do you do with the old system while you're building the new one? Some organizations choose to put the old system on "maintenance mode" and give it only the resources for patches and fixes necessary to keep the lights on. If the new project falls behind schedule (and it almost certainly will), the old system continues to degrade. If the new project fails and is subsequently canceled, the gap between the old system and operational excellence has widened significantly in the meantime.

The longer the new system takes to get up and running, the longer users and the business side of the organization have to wait for new features. Neglecting business needs breaks trust with engineering, making it more difficult for engineering to secure resources in the future.

On the other hand, if you continue development on the old system while building a new system, keeping design decisions in sync between the two teams is a considerable challenge. If those systems handle data, and almost all computer systems do, migrating the data over from one to another poses a huge challenge.

Another consideration is the people involved. Who gets to work on the new system, and who takes on the maintenance tasks of the old system? If the old system is written in an obsolete technology relevant only to that particular system, the team maintaining the old system is essentially sitting around waiting to be fired. And don't kid yourself, they know it. So if the people maintaining the old system are not participating in the creation of the new system, you should expect that they are also looking for new jobs. If they leave before your new system is operational, you lose both their expertise and their institutional knowledge.

That being said, lots of little parts within a big modernization project are not improved much by any kind of iteration. If you have an interface written in ActionScript, it's probably better to just rewrite it and push it into production as a full replacement.

Iteration in Place

If you have a working system, sometimes the simplest thing to do is to iterate it until it looks the way you want. This works well with managing technical debt, but you can also use it for situations when you want to redo the architecture. A fair amount of prep work is necessary to make iteration in place work. You will need to set up monitoring. At a minimum, you should have some way to track errors in the application layer and search logs, but the tooling here grows more sophisticated every year. The better you can identify what normal looks like on your legacy system, the easier it is to iterate in place safely.

Another area to make sure you have a mature approach is testing. Tests should run automatically, without needing a human being to follow test cases manually. Tests should also be multilevel, testing both the small units of code and whole processes end to end. Good tests take skill to write, and entire books have been written on the subject, so I won't attempt to summarize them in a few paragraphs here. The most relevant guide for legacy modernizations is Michael Feathers' *Working Effectively with Legacy Code*.

Finally, make sure your team can recover from failures quickly. This is an engineering best practice generally, but it's especially important if you're making changes to production systems. If you've never restored from a backup, you don't actually have backups. If you've never failed over to another region, you don't actually have failovers. If you've never rolled back a deploy, you don't have a mature deploy pipeline.

If you have a good monitoring strategy, have a good testing strategy, and can roll back changes quickly, you will be able to change almost anything about your legacy system with confidence.

Although it might seem risky, consider iteration in place to be the default approach. It is most likely to produce successful results in the greatest number of situations.

Split in Place

Split in place is a variant of iteration in place specific to breaking up systems. This can mean moving from a monolithic structure to a service-oriented one, but it can also mean taking two components that are tightly coupled and uncoupling them. The difference from iteration in place is that you finish splitting things off by integrating them back. In other words, when you pull off a service from a monolith, that service will likely still need to receive inputs from and send outputs to the monolith. So you build the separate service and ultimately connect it to the monolith before moving on to the next service. You keep doing this over and over (breaking off services and integrating them back) until you've broken the whole project into small service-based sets of code.

Blue-Green

A familiar pattern for deploys, the *blue-green technique* involves running two components in parallel and slowly draining traffic off from one and over to the other. The big benefit to doing this is that it's easy to undo if something goes wrong. Often with technology, increasing load reveals problems that were not otherwise found in testing. Legacy systems have both the blessing and the curse of an existing pool of users and activity. The system that replaces them has a narrow grace period with which to fix those mistakes discovered under high load. Blue-green deployments allow the new system to ease into the full load of the old system gradually, and you can fix problems before the load exacerbates them.

The Hard Cutoff

The *hard cutoff* is a deployment strategy where the new system or component replaces the old all at once. It is one of the riskiest strategies in the modernization toolbox.

A hard cutoff is sometimes done in stages, usually by environment or region. An organization might deploy to a low-traffic region first, monitor for issues, and then deploy to a higher-traffic region. This gives the organization some of the benefits of blue-green deploys in that it can stop the update (and ideally roll it back) midstream, but this method is not as accurate as blue-green deploys. The difference between environments and regions might not be completely predictable, and problems might escape notice.

If you don't have multiple regions or are working with software designed to be installed by the user and have no control over how many users get access to the new version, you may not have a choice. Alpha and beta testing groups help in the latter case; making sure you can undo any change (either through restoring from backup or reverting/rolling back commands in the version control system) helps in the former case.

Putting It Together

Good planning is less about controlling every detail and more about setting expectations across the organization. Your plan will define what it means to modernize your legacy system, what the goals are, and what value will be delivered and when. Specifically, your plan should focus on answering the following questions:

- What problem are we trying to solve by modernizing?
- What small pragmatic changes will help us learn more about the system?

- What can we iterate on?

- How will we spot problems after we deploy changes?

Next, we'll look at how to move out of the planning stage and into facing the problems that will make implementation hard.

WHY IS IT HARD?

On the surface, each legacy modernization project starts off feeling easy. After all, a working system did exist at one point. Somehow the organization managed to figure out enough to put something into production and keep it running for years. All the modernizing team should need to do is simply repeat that process using better technology, the benefit of hindsight, and improved tooling. It should be easy.

But, because people do not see the hidden technical challenges they are about to uncover, they also assume the work will be boring. There's little glory to be had reimplementing a solved problem. An organization about to embark on such an undertaking craves new features, new functionality, and new benefits. Modernization projects are typically the ones organizations just want to get out of the way, so they usually launch into them unprepared for the time and resource commitments they require.

I tell my engineers that the biggest problems we have to solve are not technical problems, but people problems. Modernization projects take months, if not years of work. Keeping a team of engineers focused, inspired, and motivated from beginning to end is difficult. Keeping their senior leadership prepared to invest over and over on what is, in effect, something they already have is a huge challenge. Creating momentum and sustaining it are where most modernization projects fail.

By far, the biggest momentum killers are the assumptions that tell us the project should be easy in the first place. They are, in no particular order, the following:

- We can build on the lessons learned from the old system.
- We understand the boundaries on the old system.
- We can use tools to speed things up.

Let's take a little time discussing why these obvious truths might not be as useful as they seem.

The Curse of Hindsight

In poker, people call it *resulting*. It's the habit of confusing the quality of the outcome with the quality of the decision. In psychology, people call it a *self-serving bias*. When things go well, we overestimate the roles of skill and ability and underestimate the role of luck. When things go poorly, on the other hand, it's all bad luck or external forces.

One of the main reasons legacy modernization projects are hard is because people overvalue the hindsight an existing system offers them. They assume that the existing system's success was a matter of skill and that they discovered all the potential problems and resolved them the best possible way in the process of building it initially. They look at the results and don't pay any attention to the quality of the decisions or the elements of luck that produced those results.

Of course, more often than not, very little documentation regarding the original decisions remains for them to study in the first place. Still, overlooking the role that plain luck plays in the success of any project means the team thinks they have room for extra innovations on top of the original challenge.

Software can have serious bugs and still be wildly successful. Lotus 1-2-3 famously mistook 1900 for a leap year, but it was so popular that versions of Excel to this day have to be programmed to honor that mistake to ensure backward compatibility. And because Excel's popularity ultimately dwarfed that of Lotus 1-2-3, the bug is now part of the ECMA Office Open XML specification.

Success and quality are not necessarily connected. Legacy systems are successful systems, but that does not mean every decision made in designing and implementing them was the right decision. Most people think they know that, but they go in the wrong direction with it. They're cynical about the system, but despite that, they overload the road map with new features and functionality. No matter how critical of the system they appear to be, they still assume the underlying problem has been solved.

We struggle to modernize legacy systems because we fail to pay the proper attention and respect to the real challenge of legacy systems: the context has been lost. We have forgotten the web of compromises that created the final design and are blind to the years of modifications that increased its complexity. We don't realize that at least a few design choices were bad choices and that it was only through good luck the system performed well for so long. We oversimplify and ultimately commit to new challenges before we discover our mistakes.

Being dismissive of legacy systems is no guarantee that we won't also fall into the trap of relying on context that is lost. Remember the game I described in Chapter 3 when looking at what parts of the system shouldn't be in COBOL? It's a useful technique even when COBOL is not a factor. By challenging my team to design a system with the same requirements of our legacy system using only technology available at the time the legacy system was built, we're forced to recover some context. Many of the "stupid" technical choices from the legacy system seem very different. Once forced to look directly at the context, we realize how innovative some of those systems really were. This gives us a little insight into which decisions were skill and foresight and which were luck.

A successful system could have a design pattern that will not survive past a certain scale of usage but that was able to achieve its operational goals without ever crossing that threshold. Is that skill or luck? If the designers knew the system would not scale but also knew the system would never reach the point where it would need to scale that way, we could assume the design was a deliberate decision. For example, perhaps the system is accessible only to certain people for internal purposes. Scaling to millions of requests was not necessary, because it would only ever get hundreds of requests per second at most.

On the other hand, if the system was designed with the idea that its usage would continue to grow indefinitely and the designers chose a pattern that will survive only up to a certain point, their success is a matter of luck. They simply did not reach that tipping point. Twitter was a well-designed system until it became so popular it started falling apart, serving users the notorious "fail whale" cartoon instead of their content. Overnight, the engineers who built the social media platform and the technology it used went from being perceived as skillful operators with superior code to a bunch of rank amateurs with an overhyped, dumbed-down programming language. They were neither geniuses nor dummies.

Scale always involves some luck. You can plan for a certain number of transactions or users, but you can't really control those factors, especially if you're building anything that involves the public internet. Software systems tend to incorporate multiple technologies working together to complete some task. I don't know anyone who can predict how multiple technologies will behave in every potential scale condition, especially not when they are combined. Engineering teams do their best to mitigate potential problems, but they will never be able to foresee every possible combination of events. For that reason, whether a service works at its initial scale and then continues to work as it grows is always a mix of skill and luck.

Easy and Also Impossible

In 1988, computer scientist Hans Moravec observed that it was really hard to teach computers to do very basic things, but it was much easier to program computers to do seemingly complex things. Skills that had been evolving for thousands of years to solve problems like walking, answering questions, and identifying objects were intuitive, subconscious, and impossibly difficult to teach a computer how to do. Meanwhile skills that had not been a part of the human experience for thousands of years— like playing chess or geolocation—were relatively straightforward. His theory connecting this paradox to evolution, which had been observed by other contemporaneous AI researchers, gained enough traction that the paradox itself was named after him.

In Moravec's own words, "It is comparatively easy to make computers exhibit adult-level performance on intelligence tests or playing checkers, and difficult or impossible to give them the skills of a one-year-old when it comes to perception and mobility."[1]

Those wishing to upgrade large complex systems would do well to keep Moravec's paradox in mind. Systems evolve much faster than nature, but just as in nature, as the system evolves, more and more of its underlying logic becomes obscured. When we get used to something just working a certain way, we tend to forget about it. Once we've stopped thinking about it, we fail to factor it into our plans to modernize.

We assume that successful systems solved their core problems well, but we also assume things that just work without any thought or effort

---

[1] Hans Moravec, *Mind Children: The Future of Robot and Human Intelligence* (Cambridge, MA: Harvard University Press, 1988), 15.

are simple when they may in fact bear the complexity of years of iteration we've forgotten about.

This is especially true when the system has multiple layers of abstraction and even more so when those abstractions grow past the application boundaries itself—when they leverage operating system APIs or even hardware interfaces. When was the last time you thought about whether your favorite software is compatible with the chip architecture on your computer? When was the last time you needed to hunt down a specific driver to get a new accessory to work with your operating system? If you were born after the 1990s, you might never have thought about these things at all. Hardware and software interfaces haven't gotten simpler in the last two decades, we've just abstracted away a lot of annoying differences that made the issue of x86 versus x64 or downloading drivers a normal part of working even casually with computers.

With very old legacy systems, the abstraction layers might not be there, or worse, they themselves might be out-of-date. I like to call this problem *overgrowth*, and it's worth describing in detail.

Overgrowth: The Application and Its Dependencies

Overgrowth is a particular type of coupling between the software and the layers of abstraction making up the platform on which it runs. The perils of dependency management are well known, but with legacy systems, dependency management is about more than just what a package manager might install. The older a system is, the more likely the platform on which it runs is itself a dependency. Most modernization projects do not think about the platform this way and, therefore, leave the issue as an unpleasant surprise to be discovered later.

We've made huge leaps in cross-compatibility, but we've not yet reached the state where applications are 100 percent platform-agnostic, nor are we ever likely to achieve that completely.

For that reason, we cannot modernize a system without considering the underlying platform. Which features of that platform are unique, and which are found in other options? How old is the platform, and has it since been supplanted by a completely different way of doing things?

What makes major migrations so tricky is that as software ages, elements of the platform on which it was defined to run fall out of fashion, and support for those elements on other platforms becomes less and less common. This means that on our oldest systems, there is typically logic that either must be written out of the system or must be reproduced on a modern platform. The existing platform becomes auxiliary software that grows around whatever is being migrated. If you're switching databases, for example, you're not just moving the data. You might have to rewrite your queries in a different language or a different implementation of SQL. You may need to rethink hooks or stored procedures. One software language often has any number of minor languages that facilitate specific functions. There are command processors like bash or JCL that trigger jobs, templating languages to build interfaces, querying languages to access data, and so on. How well is business logic separated out between these layers? Does logic stay where it is sensible, or is it injected to where it is convenient?

Most web development projects, for example, run on Linux machines. Therefore, it is not uncommon for web applications to include shell scripts as part of their code base—particularly as part of the setup/installation routine. Imagine what migrating those applications would feel like 20 years in the future if Linux were supplanted by a different operating system. We would potentially have to rewrite all the shell scripts as well as migrate the actual application.

Smart engineers will point out that with containerization and configuration management tools, such scripts should be a thing of the past, but that's precisely why overgrowth is an issue for legacy code. At one point, doing certain tasks via shell script was commonplace; this has since been overtaken by a different approach. If we want to migrate an older application, we may find that this older approach is not supported by the technology we want to use. We must migrate the auxiliary software first.

For modern applications, overgrowth is not usually a significant blocker. Languages from the same general era of computing tend to share ecosystems, so it is easier to pull out one language and replace it with another while making only minimum changes to the auxiliary software around it. Remember, overgrowth is just another form of coupling. Coupling is not necessarily a bad thing if the value add is there.

In older applications, however, people seem to have trouble seeing where this type of coupling is. We tend to forget about auxiliary software, just as we forget the complex processes behind the simple tasks Moravec struggled to program computers to do. The longer a piece goes without being upgraded, the less likely modern platforms and tools will support it. As auxiliary software slides out of support, the challenge of modernizing the actual code becomes more complicated.

Look for overgrowth at integration points, places where the communication layer changes. There are a few different transitions where you are likely to find it.

Shifting Vertically: Moving from One Abstraction Layer to Another

Many layers exist between modern software and the physical voltage moving through circuits in a machine. On the most basic level, we can define three layers: the software, the hardware, and an operating system between them. Overgrowth when shifting up or down these layers typically takes the form of proprietary standards, especially with older technology where the manufacturer of the hardware would also provide the software. Look out for situations where your application code depends on APIs specific to your operating system or, worse, when it's specific to the chip architecture of the physical machine on which it runs. This was a common problem with old mainframes. Software was written in a variant of Assembly specific to both the company that built the mainframe and usually the model of the machine itself.

Shifting Horizontally: Moving from One Application to Another

Just as there is legacy code, there are also legacy protocols. When two applications pass data back and forth between each other, if they are running on machines or communicating on networking equipment developed by a corporation with proprietary protocols, you may see some overgrowth around the connection. This is less of a concern with web development, because the decentralized nature of the internet pushed things toward standard protocols like TCP/IP, FTP, and SMTP—all of which have a robust ecosystem of tooling and broad support across multiple platforms. In other areas of software development, proprietary protocols have a larger footprint. How difficult these protocols are depends on how common the technology in question is. Proprietary protocols from large vendors are probably supported by other options. For example, Microsoft Exchange Server protocols are proprietary but well supported, while an application dependent on AppleTalk might prove difficult to migrate.

Shifting from Client to Server

This shift can take the form of specific software development kits (SDKs) for specific tools and integrations, drivers for specific database connections, or frontend to backend movement. It might horrify some engineers to know this, but internal web applications are still sometimes built to run on certain web browsers and rely on features or functions not available in others. Internet Explorer is the most likely culprit. Whenever you see IE as the preferred default browser for internal applications, double-check that the frontend of these applications is not using IE-specific JavaScript features. We also see this frequently with Adobe Acrobat. Early-generation digital forms frequently were built to leverage Acrobat-specific PDF features and may be difficult to move between versions of Acrobat. A famous story about this comes from my time at

US Digital Service where one of the Department of Veterans Affairs' websites refused to work unless you *downgraded* your version of Acrobat.[2]

Shifting Down the Dependency Tree

As programming languages mature, they occasionally introduce breaking changes to their syntax or internal logic. Not all dependencies upgrade to handle those changes at the same pace, creating a mess where the application cannot be upgraded until the dependencies are upgraded. In applications that are very old, it is likely that some of those dependencies are no longer in active development. For instance, perhaps the maintainers never rolled out a version that is compatible with the newest version of Java or Node.js, and to get that support, the application must switch to a completely different option.

Cutting Back the Overgrowth

Cutting back overgrowth is not technically hard; it is just frustrating and demoralizing. Overgrowth slows things down, and if not accurately assessed, it creates unfortunate surprises that affect a team's confidence. To minimize its impact, start off by mapping the application's context. What does it run on? What is the process around creating a new instance of it? Map its dependencies two levels down.[3] Attempt to trace the flow of data through the application to complete one request. This should give you a clearer picture of where there are likely to be problems. If you can put these problems on a road map, they have less dramatic impact on morale.

---

[2] "Matt Cutts on the US Digital Service and Working at Google for 17 Years," *Y Combinator*, December 4, 2019, *https://blog.ycombinator.com/matt-cutts-on-the-us-digital-service-and-working-at-google-for-17-years/*.

[3] Dependency trees can be quite complicated, and traversing the whole graph is a lot of work without a lot of payoff. Make a list of the application's direct dependencies and what those packages depend on, and then accept the risk that there might be a problem in nodes further down and move on.

You might be tempted to think that modern software development is improving this situation. Cross-compatibility is much better than it used to be, that's true, but the growth of the platform as a service (PaaS) market for commercial cloud is increasing the options to program for specific platform features. For example, the more you build things with Amazon's managed services, the more the application will conform to fit Amazon-specific characteristics, and the more overgrowth there will be to contend with if the organization later wants to migrate away.

Automation and Conversion

The last assumption people make about legacy systems is that because computers can read the code they are trying to modernize, there must be some way to automate the process. They introduce tools like transpilers and static analysis with the intention of making modernization faster and more efficient.

Those tools are useful, but only if the expectations for them are realistic. If you use them as guides to help inform the process, your modernization team can move strategically, side-stepping critical mistakes and maybe reducing some costs. However, if you use them as shortcuts and skimp on making a true investment in modernization, they will likely let you down. Organizations that think the tools are the solution typically end up with longer, more painful, and more expensive modernizations.

So, what do these tools do exactly, and what's the right way to use them?

Transpiling Code

Transpiling is the process of automatically translating code written in one programming language into another programming language. It makes sense to use a transpiler when the difference between the language being read and the language in which the output will be written is not significant. For example, Python version 3 had enough breaking changes in it that the transition actually required engineers to migrate their code bases rather than simply upgrade them. At the same time, Python 3 did not change any of the fundamental philosophies of Python itself, just some implementation details. Transpiling worked so well that tools for Python 2 to Python 3 conversion and Python 3 to Python 2 conversion are now built in to Python 3.

Another great use case for transpilers is when the language that the transpiler is reading was specifically designed to enforce good practices on the language the transpiler is writing. JavaScript has many different variants of this approach, such as CoffeeScript and TypeScript.

When the differences between the input and output languages are significant, transpiling becomes more problematic, and time-saving expectations need to be managed properly to ensure a successful outcome. The classic example of this use case is COBOL to Java. COBOL is procedural, imperative, and fixed-point by default. Java is object-oriented and floating-point by default. Transpiling COBOL to Java may produce code that works, but it will not be maintainable unless engineers go over the code and fine-tune it. Often this means rewriting parts of it.

If you are going to use a transpiler for that kind of upgrade, it is absolutely essential that the application has well-designed and comprehensive test suites, preferably automated ones. The bugs created by automatically translating one language to another, completely different language can be subtle and difficult to track down. For example, when you try to put an eight-digit number into a variable defined as having seven digits, COBOL truncates the last digit and moves on. Java, on the other hand, throws an exception. The transpiler will not add code to handle these exceptions.

People often invest in transpilers to help upgrade their legacy code because they think it will save engineering time to have a computer program do the first pass, or they think it will replace the need for experts in the original language to assist altogether. But when the two languages have significant differences, the output of such transpilers doesn't usually follow the structure and conventions of the language in which it writes. Transpilers are not capable of rethinking how you organize your code. Transpiled COBOL is Java written as if it were COBOL, and therefore, it's unintelligible to most Java programmers.

The success stories around this kind of transpiling typically come from companies that use their transpiling solution as a gateway to consulting services. That is to say, first you buy licenses to use the transpiler, and then you buy the talent to rewrite the transpiler's output into something workable. This is a fine strategy, as long as you know that's what you're getting into.

Static Analysis

Although it hasn't gained much traction outside a theoretical context, some interesting work in academia has been done around deploying various forms of static analysis to explore and ultimately improve legacy systems. So-called software renovation combines techniques from compiler design and reverse engineering to steer the refactoring process. Software renovation is intended to be semi-automatic: the analysis is automatic, but software engineers do the actual work of restructuring the code.

Some common types of static analysis used for software renovation include the following:

DEPENDENCY GRAPHS In this style of software renovation, the dependency graph is mapped, and clustering algorithms are used to determine where there is overlap, redundancy, unused libraries, or circular dependencies.[4]

GRAMMARS These are language-specific tools that produce analysis by parsing the abstract syntax tree. Typically they look for

---

[4.] Massimiliano Di Penta, Markus Neteler, Giuliano Antoniol, and E. Merlo, "A Language-Independent Software Renovation Framework," *Journal of Systems and Software* 77, no. 3 (September 2005): 225–240.

duplicate code or specific practices that are considered anti-patterns (like goto statements).

CONTROL FLOW/DATA FLOW GRAPHS   These graphs are tools that track how software executes. Control flow graphs map the order in which lines of code are executed, while data flow graphs map the variable assignments and references. You can use such analysis to discover lost business requirements or track down dead code.

Software renovation methodology hasn't quite broken out of theoretical studies, but static analysis tools are available both as stand-alone products and as features of larger integrated development environments or continuous integration and deployment solutions. This is unfortunate because the methodology is what drives the bulk of the impact. The tools themselves are not as important as the phases of excavating, understanding, documenting, and ultimately rewriting and replacing legacy systems. Tools will come and go.

A Guide to Not Making Things Harder

Expectation management is really important. Typically organizations make the mistakes described in this chapter because they believe they are making the process more efficient. They misjudge how long modernization projects take, and they misjudge how much time they can save and how to save it.

Modernization projects have better outcomes when we replace the false assumptions described at the opening of this chapter with the following guidelines:

- Keep it simple. Don't add new problems to solve just because the old system was successful. Success does not mean the old system completely solved its problem. Some of those technical decisions were wrong, but never caused any problems.

- Spend some time trying to recover context. Treat the platform as a dependency and look for coupling that won't transfer easily to a modern platform.

- Tools and automation should supplement human effort, not replace it.

Individual contributors often find the barrier to following that advice is not convincing themselves, but convincing others. Particularly when the organization is big, the pressure to run projects the same way everyone else does, so that they look correct even at the expense of being successful, is significant. In later chapters, we'll tackle navigating the organization and strategies to advance your goals.

BUILDING AND
PROTECTING MOMENTUM

This book mainly focuses on big projects. When I discuss upgrades, I'm not talking about running a package manager to install the latest versions of your dependencies. When I mention deprecations, I'm not talking about versioning your API. Much of the advice in this book will work regardless of project size, but it is primarily intended for big ones.

Chapter 3 covered developing strategy around the engineering challenge posed by your legacy system. In that chapter, I described the shape and nature of different types of approaches and how to look at such a challenge holistically. This chapter describes a similar approach from the organizational side: how to create a plan that builds momentum and keeps teams focused and optimistic even as the work becomes difficult.

The funny thing about big legacy modernization projects is that technologists suddenly seem drawn to strategies that they know do not work in other contexts. Few modern software engineers would forgo Agile development to spend months planning exactly what an architecture should look like and try to build a complete product all at once. And yet, when asked to modernize an old system, suddenly everyone is breaking things down into sequential phases that are completely dependent on one another.

Agile approaches to legacy challenges are not well publicized. Any number of books are available that describe how you build software. A few exist that cover how to maintain software, and even fewer have been published that explain how to tackle the challenges of rebuilding software when it has been left to rot or was built wrong in the first place.

In truth, what works when rebuilding a system is not all that different from what worked to build it in the first place. You need to keep the scope small, and you need to iterate on your successes. This might seem unnecessary, because the old system and its history have defined all your requirements for you. Assuming you fully understand the requirements because an existing system is operational is a critical mistake. One of the advantages of building a new system is that the team is more aware of the unknowns. Existing systems can be a distraction. The software team treats the full-featured implementation of it as the MVP, no matter how large or how complex that existing system actually is. It's simply too much information to manage. People become overwhelmed, and they get discouraged and demoralized. The project stalls and reinforces the notion that the modernization work is impossible.

Momentum Builder: The Bliss of Measurable Problems

There are a couple different ways to restrict scope when an existing system looms in the background. The most straightforward approach is to define an MVP from the existing system's array of features. Pare it down into a lighter-weight version of itself that becomes the first iteration and then gradually add back features. While sensible, this strategy requires discipline and strong leadership. All users of the existing system will naturally see the features they use as the most critical and lobby to get them scheduled for the earliest possible iteration. The process becomes political very quickly.

Instead, I prefer to restrict the scope by defining one measurable problem we are trying to solve. Building a modern infrastructure is not a goal. Different people naturally are going to disagree on which standards and best practices should be enforced and on how strongly they should be enforced. Few real-life systems completely conform to an ideal; there are always at least one or two places in systems where a nonstandard approach was used to make a specific function or integration work. Everyone knows these compromises exist and that they probably will continue to exist in some form or another in the new system, but it's unlikely the organization will be able to agree on when and where to introduce them.

But if all the work is structured around one critical problem that you can measure and monitor, these conversations become much easier. You start by looking for as many opportunities as possible to make the problem better and prioritize them by amount of estimated impact. When there is a disagreement on approach or technology, the criteria for the decision becomes "Which one moves the needle further?"

Legacy modernization projects go better when the individuals contributing to them feel comfortable being autonomous and when they can adapt to challenges and surprises as they present themselves because they understand what the priorities are. The more decisions need to go up to a senior group—be that VPs, enterprise architects, or a CEO—the more delays and bottlenecks appear. The more momentum is lost, and people stop believing success is possible. When people stop believing success is possible, they stop bringing their best to work. Measurable problems empower team members to make decisions. Everyone has agreed that metric X needs to be better; any actions taken to improve metric X need not be run up the chain of command.

Measurable problems create clearly articulated goals. Having a goal means you can define what kind of value you expect the project to add and whom that value will benefit most. Will modernization make things faster for customers? Will it improve scaling so you can sign bigger clients? Will it save people's lives? Or, will it just mean that someone gets to give a conference talk or write an article about switching from technology A to technology B?

Anatomy of the Measurable Problem

It's natural to want to approach architecture in a holistic way. Our minds love order and patterns, the neatness of everything being consistent and well thought out. But systems are like houses; they never really stay perfectly clean for long. The very act of using something forces it to change. You have less memory and less storage, your hardware decays, and you've added new features, which mean more lines of code.

Good modernization work needs to suppress that impulse to create elegant comprehensive architectures up front. You can have your neat and orderly system, but you won't get it from designing it that way in the beginning. Instead, you'll build it through iteration.

The measurable problem is what will guide your teams through the modernization effort. When the legacy system was new, its footprint and the team that ran it were both small. As the system grew, internal politics grew with it. In some cases, entire business units were born or rearranged to follow the pattern of the technology. Getting all those people to agree and march in the same direction is difficult. The strength of the measurable problem is that it is objective and irrefutable, and therefore, it helps the team navigate the internal politics they have inherited from the existing system. People can and will disagree on whether the measurable problem is the right problem to solve, but that shifts the burden of mediating those disagreements away from the engineering team and toward the senior executive who signed off on focusing modernization activities on that measurable problem in the first place.

The last benefit of measurable problems is that positive results are not linked to feature launches. When the team tries to create an MVP from an existing system, the organization will pressure them to achieve feature parity with the existing system as quickly as possible. Success or failure becomes tied to launches, which encourages cut corners and technical debt.

In all likelihood, the business side of the organization does not understand what's wrong with the existing system. Rolling out features they already have is not something they will celebrate. To build momentum behind a modernization effort, it's essential to communicate how modernizing will improve the status quo. Defining a measurable problem explains to the business side of the organization how the existing system could be better. Once the metrics and criteria are defined, any given action either moves the needle in a positive direction or doesn't. Missteps are easier to identify, define, and correct. Everyone in the organization can figure out how things are going by looking at the metrics.

But how does one identify a good measurable problem?

The easiest candidates are ones that reflect the business or mission goals of the organization. If you're thinking about rearchitecting a system and cannot tie the effort back to some kind of business goal, you probably shouldn't be doing it at all.

When I was working for the government, one of the most inspiring projects I saw was the effort to modernize the immigration system enough to meet a stretch goal for refugee resettlement the Obama administration had set. The system itself, even just the subset that concerned refugees, was large and complex. Engineers were overwhelmed by the scope of it and the problems that it experienced from time to time.

But the challenge of this particular project was not to make that whole system better; it was to get that whole system to process a specific type of application faster. Defining the goal in this way created a much clearer scope for the effort. The team started by doing an analysis of where the bottlenecks in application processing were, and then they began precision-targeting those areas, seeking only to make iterative improvements. Conversations about prioritization focused on what changes were likely to increase the number of applications processed—numbers anyone on the team could look at and refer to as needed. As they worked toward this specific goal, the team passed up a lot of opportunities to make much needed infrastructure changes, because doing so would not produce the results where they needed them.

At first glance, this approach might seem unwise or even irresponsible, but the number-one killer of big efforts is not technical failure. It's loss of momentum. To be successful at those long-term rearchitecting challenges, the team needs to establish a feedback loop that continuously builds on and promotes their track record of success. When it became clear that the refugee team was not only going to reach the stretch goal—a number that many felt was impossible—but that they were actually going to overshoot it by a few thousand people, other teams that were better positioned to make those much needed infrastructure changes started coming to work with renewed energy. Don't lose sight of the fact that modernization projects are long and typically involve coordinating multiple teams. Being strategically narrow-minded to demonstrate value and build momentum is not a bad idea.

Good measurable problems have to be focused on problems that your engineers give a shit about. Number of refugees saved from ISIS was an easy goal to rally people around. In all likelihood, you won't be able to say your database migration is going to do that, but engineers feel passionate about other things. Talk to them and figure out what those are.

Momentum Killer: The Team Cannot Agree

When I moved from being an individual contributor to running engineering teams, my role in technical conversations shifted. I saw better outcomes when I focused on facilitating a productive conversation rather than vying to be the decision-maker. Have you ever found yourself in a meeting that felt like it was running around in circles? Meetings where people seemed to be competing to see who could predict the most obscure potential failure? Meetings where past decisions were relitigated and everyone walked away less certain as to what the next steps were? Facilitating technical conversations is more important than being the decision-maker because unproductive and frustrating meetings demoralize teams.

Because large systems are typically complex, out of control meetings can derail decision-making about the technology that backs them. Measurable problems help people prioritize what improvements to make and in which order, but when it comes to the nitty-gritty implementation details, it is not always possible to predict which options will have the biggest impact. Reasonable people are going to disagree, but pointless arguments need to be defused before they do too much damage.

Step 1: Define a Scope

The best way to handle dysfunctional decision-making meetings is to prevent them from happening in the first place by defining and enforcing a scope. I usually start meetings by listing the desired outcomes, the outcomes I would be satisfied with, and what's out of scope for this decision. I may even write this information on a whiteboard or put it in a PowerPoint slide for reference. What do we want to accomplish in this meeting? If we get stuck, what other outcomes would be acceptable? Sometimes a team cannot agree because there is an actual blocker to agreement—a gray area that requires more research, for example. If that happens, what is the smallest decision we could make and still feel like the meeting was productive?

Once the meeting has a scope, I define areas that we should be able to agree are outside that scope. Often out-of-scope issues are decisions that are neither blockers nor dependencies. The hard ones do seem to be related to in-scope issues, so when in doubt, the team needs to be able to articulate clearly how our in-scope decisions are affected by the issue being raised. For example, I had an engineering team that was charged with creating a seamless platform where engineers could run commands and have the heavy lifting of building, configuring, and deploying done for them. At the same time, the organization was also thinking about phasing out one programming language in favor of another. To accomplish the first goal, we needed to make a few decisions about the architecture of the tool. Would we build a suite of separate tools, or would we build one tool that we could add functionality to? Whatever design pattern we chose could have been done equally well in either language, so any debate about programming languages would bring us no closer to reaching a decision on what we wanted the meeting to be about. Discussions about programming languages were out of scope. Although the issue would ultimately affect implementation of the design pattern we selected, it was neither a blocker nor a dependency when picking the pattern.

With my engineers, I set the expectation that to have a productive, free-flowing debate, we need to be able to sort comments and issues into in-scope and out-of-scope quickly and easily as a team. I call this technique "true but irrelevant," because I can typically sort meeting information into three buckets: things that are true, things that are false, and things that are true but irrelevant. Irrelevant is just a punchier way of saying out of scope.

The purpose of thinking about comments made during meetings as true, false, or true but irrelevant is not to discourage people from bringing up irrelevant details. When we think of contributions only in terms of true or false, we put pressure on individuals to save face by fighting to have the validity of their irrelevant facts acknowledged. By encouraging people to think about their comments as in-scope and out-of-scope, we're saying that the engineer speaking raised a valid point that should be considered in a different conversation.

At the same time, relevancy is often difficult for any one person to determine. You don't want engineers to self-censor for fear of bringing up something that's out of scope. They might incorrectly assume something is out of scope because they have incomplete information. If they fail to raise the issue because they associate the true but irrelevant bucket with failure, they may fail to point out actual problems. A great meeting is not a meeting where no one ever mentions anything out of scope; it's one where out-of-scope comments are quickly identified as such by the team and dispatched before they have derailed the conversation.

Step 2: Check for Conflicting Optimization Strategies

Even with a carefully defined scope, engineers might bump heads anyway. A quick trick when two capable engineers cannot seem to agree on a decision is to ask yourself what each one is optimizing for with their suggested approach. Remember, technology has a number of trade-offs where optimizing for one characteristic diminishes another important characteristic. Examples include security versus usability, coupling versus complexity, fault tolerance versus consistency, and so on, and so forth. If two engineers really can't agree on a decision, it's usually because they have different beliefs about where the ideal optimization between two such poles is.

Looking for absolute truths in situations that are ambiguous and value-based is painful. Sometimes it helps just to highlight the fact that the disagreement is really over what to optimize for, rather than pure technical correctness. What is the impact of each optimization? Can the negative effects of over-optimizing in one direction be mitigated?

Step 3: Perform Time-Boxed Experiments

If the disagreement is in scope and isn't a matter of conflicting optimization strategies, the best way to settle it is by creating time-boxed experiments. Find a way to try each approach on a small sample size with a clear evaluation date and specific success criteria defined in advance. Becoming good at experiments is valuable for practically any organization. It's the basis of iteration—you build something, collect data on how it is performing, modify it to improve performance, and start the cycle over. This is how effective technology is built, so engineering teams should get comfortable using it to make hard decisions.

Momentum Killer: A History of Failure

Odds are good that the modernization effort you're working on now is not the first attempt. Companies that successfully maintain their technology over time usually do not need to engage in a big modernization project after all. They are able to keep up through incremental change and regular maintenance. If you are running a team tasked with just cleaning up the debt and migrating onto more suitable technologies, it means the existing organization has failed to adapt.

Your specific situation might have a history of failure that is much deeper than slacking off on regular maintenance. Is this even the first modernization project? If not, each prior effort likely has left scar tissue on the organization that you need to consider. The more false starts a project has had, the harder it is to build the momentum necessary to succeed.

The first deliverables of a modernization effort have to take this history of failure into account. People aren't pessimistic and uninspired by legacy modernization projects because they don't care or don't realize that modernization is important. They often feel that way because they are convinced that success is impossible after experiencing a number of failures.

At the same time, I have yet to find a group of engineers who didn't want to believe they could reach a better state. It's surprisingly easy to change people's minds about the inevitability of failure when you demonstrate that success is possible.

Inspired and motivated engineering teams run smoother and more productive modernization processes, so design your modernization strategy around front-loading value. What changes will produce the most immediate positive impact?

I once worked for an organization that was facing a major challenge around the breakup of its monolith. The organization wanted to build a standardized platform that product engineering teams could use to deploy services to production easily—a reasonable ambition—but the product itself was three monoliths crammed onto a single VM. It was a monolith of monoliths, if you will. At the time it had been built, that architecture fit the business case, but in the years that followed, the organization had seen explosive growth. By the time I got there, the architecture didn't make sense anymore.

This organization was facing two problems. First, the platform initiative and the monolith breakup were blocking each other. The product teams did not want to break up their monolith into services until they could deploy on a platform. Understandably, they did not want to put something on a release pipeline only to have to migrate it off when the platform arrived. The platform group, on the other hand, could not build a platform without requirements set by the product teams. They had to be able to build with the real needs of real services in mind—services that did not exist because they had not been broken off the monolith yet.

The second problem was that the organization had actually tried both sides of this process before and failed at them, multiple times. It had tried to build a platform and had migrated some small, unimportant services that could be split off with minimum redesign. It had tried this at least three times by my estimation, each time losing momentum and failing to finish.

The organization had also tried to break up the monolith several times. Each time, it became overwhelmed by the complexity of the task. Splitting monoliths is rarely, if ever, only about copying and pasting some code into a different repository. When software is designed to be coupled, engineers usually take advantage of that fact and build on the easy access that coupling provides. In this case, that meant their testing suites had a high concentration of end-to-end tests over unit tests.

It meant multiple components were accessing the same data store and sharing responsibilities over the same information. When their tightly coupled monolith became decoupled services, the tests would break, and a plan for keeping the data consistent between services would need to be developed.

Now facing their fourth attempt, optimism was pretty low. Everybody wanted to see the project be successful, but no one wanted to be the first team to invest the work only to be left holding the bag when the effort fell apart once again.

Prominent engineers on the platform group were asked to come up with a plan. They spent weeks collecting data and interviewing teams and eventually pitched the following compromise: they would pull the three monoliths onto their own release channels with their own VMs, thereby ensuring that the platform could support everything the product needed without requiring the product team to split anything immediately.

The problem with this plan was that it didn't actually make anything better. Now instead of one release cycle with an owner and an orderly schedule determining when code hit each region and environment, the organization would have three release cycles with no one owning them. Every deploy would have to be carefully coordinated across multiple teams so that changes did not accidentally hit production for one monolith early or late.

It wasn't going to lower costs either. Commercial cloud providers charge per time usage of each VM. Three separate sets of VMs meant the proposed plan would easily double or even triple the organization's hosting expenses.

I wasn't even sure it would get off the ground. My team had been working hard redesigning a service that appeared to be fully separate to go onto the platform, and we were finding all sort of weird places where components were integrated in unexpected ways.

What was the value of putting three monoliths on separate release channels?

When I asked that question, the engineers thought I was asking what the value of breaking up the monolith was. It took several conversations before I could get them to understand that I wasn't questioning their goal. I was questioning their starting point. Starting with tripling the number of VMs would make updates more complicated for product teams and would increase spending unnecessarily. Why would the organization continue to invest in the process of breaking up the monolith if its first experiences with that process made work harder and more expensive?

The hard problems around legacy modernization are not technical problems; they're people problems. The technology is usually pretty straightforward. Keeping people focused and motivated through the months or years it takes to finish the job is hard. To do this, you need to provide significant value right away, as soon as possible, so that you overcome people's natural skepticism and get them to buy in. The important word in the phrase proof of concept is *proof*. You need to prove to people that success is possible and worth doing.

The more an organization has failed at something, the more proof it needs that modernization will bring value. When there's a history of failure, that first step has to provide enough value to build the momentum necessary to be successful. The obvious problem with that is it means there's a natural upper bound. There is a point where cynicism is so high, no single first step will ever provide enough value to prove the project will work.

Then what?

Momentum Builder: Inspiring Urgency

If you find yourself in this situation, you have a little due diligence to do first. The first question to ask is does this particular migration actually add any value at all? Or are we migrating because there's a new shiny technology in front of us? After all, monoliths are not universally bad. Plenty of successful companies run monoliths.

If you believe the migration does add value, the next question to ask yourself is will leadership make a commitment to prioritizing it? Sometimes you get lucky, and the change is one with a hard deadline and real consequences for it slipping.[1]

But if leadership isn't prioritizing it and if you believe the migration has real business value but you're weighted down with the cynicism of repeated failures, what you need is a crisis. Value is relative, after all. When things are working well and money is coming in, engineers can tolerate a multitude of sins. When things are bad, the perception of value added by nearly any change goes up. Dealing with crisis alters the organization's internal calculus around risk.

When I was working in government, we would reach the upper bound on the value scale frequently. Some of the systems were so old, efforts to modernize them had literally been passed from generation to generation. Having a crisis became an essential component of how my teams operated—to the point that we might delay talking to an agency for a few weeks or months just to see whether a crisis would pop up that we could hook into.

Occasionally, I went as far as looking for a crisis to draw attention to. This usually didn't require too much effort. Any system more than five years old will have at least a couple major things wrong with it. It didn't mean lying, and it didn't mean injecting problems where they didn't exist. Instead, it was a matter of storytelling—taking something that was unreported and highlighting its potential risks. These problems *were* problems, and my analysis of their potential impact was always truthful, but some of them could have easily stayed buried for months or years without triggering a single incident.

[1.] Alas, security certifications do have some value. Those who have them tend to like to keep them.

My favorite place to start was with security, followed by system stability. One does not need much technical literacy to understand the impact and consequences of getting those issues wrong. There are also areas where even the best technical teams struggle from time to time, so you're unlikely to come up empty-handed if you look for a potential crisis on either these two fronts.

Protecting Momentum: A Quota on Big Decisions

Now that you've done all the work of assessing the situation and organizing around it, you don't want to let the organization itself undermine that work. People mean well, but any kind of change is risky, and saying yes to risk is difficult. Never fear. You can set the stage to get a yes to organizational change rather than a no.

First, you need to learn to talk about what you are doing in a way that minimizes the number of big decisions that need to be made—particularly big decisions that include changes in process or anything that would need multiple stakeholders to sign off on and many rounds of approvals to change.

Decisions that require consulting many stakeholders are obviously difficult and painful to manage. People will naturally want to avoid them. Therefore, the more big decisions your proposal seems to include, the more likely people are going to want to slow down or delay it a quarter.

You may think that by giving projects fancy names, projecting budgets, and settling staffing questions up front you are being diligent, and you are! But you're also making the project look like a series of big decisions, which for audiences insulated from the day-to-day pain of legacy systems seems too risky. Consider different ways of talking about the same project for different audiences. Some audiences will appreciate detailed planning, and other audiences will appreciate a high-level approach.

Look for the following when you need to prune the number of big decisions that have to be made to move forward:

EXISTING PROGRAMS, PROJECTS, OR TECHNOLOGY   These are the best off-by-one errors. Riding the coattails of an already approved solution removes the need to seek out those approvals yourself.

ADVANTAGEOUS REGULATION   You can eliminate a big decision by making it seem like it was already made, but you can also eliminate a big decision by making it seem like the organization doesn't have a choice. Compliance, particularly around security, is a great place to look, because those rules often come with specific deadlines when they must be done or the organization loses certifications, funding, and, potentially, clients.

AMBIGUOUS APPROVAL PROCESS   The saying "Ask for forgiveness, not permission" is popular among the startup crowd, but let's face it, you're better off asking for forgiveness if it's believable that you might have been acting in good faith. If you're bypassing a well-documented and well-known approval process, the outcome is less likely to end favorably than when the process is ambiguous or nonexistent.

Protecting Momentum: Calculating Opportunity Costs

Value add isn't always a matter of technical outcomes. More often than not, business outcomes provide a clearer path to prioritization. Business outcomes could be profits, but if you're working for a mission-driven organization, business outcomes could also be people served or impact observed. When running a multiyear modernization project, buy-in from the business side is essential. You can't rely on them understanding the technical outcomes, so you should know how to illustrate the value of business outcomes by calculating opportunity costs.

For those not familiar with the concept, an *opportunity cost* is money lost by not doing something because you have chosen another opportunity instead. Typically, opportunity costs are expressed in expected profits not realized, but in the context of legacy systems, we usually think of opportunity costs in terms of money saved.

Opportunity costs are better as thought experiments than actual calculations. If it were possible to calculate accurately how much time and money we were going to spend on each potential approach to upgrading an existing system (or upgrading it versus leaving it be and building new features), maintaining legacy systems would be easy. But opportunity costs are useful in getting people to communicate their assumptions and build a case for why the organization should do what we want them to do. To provide value, estimates of opportunity cost need not be accurate. They need only provide insightful context of the trade-offs proposed by a given decision.

Calculating opportunity costs isn't just about making more profitable decisions. It gives the team data with which to justify the modernization activity to a wide variety of stakeholders. Investing in the health of your technology makes sense to everyone only when the technology is visibly failing, and by that point, the problem is much larger and much harder to solve. Senior management tends to be skeptical of any kind of cleanup activity—fearing that it will slow the organization's velocity unnecessarily.

My first big project at Auth0 was getting a handle on our notifications system. Auth0 was maintaining a shared email server for testing and development purposes only. Nevertheless, customers occasionally neglected to move on to a dedicated provider when going to production even though plenty of free options were available. Customers were rate-limited on the shared provider precisely because it was not intended for production, but when they hit their limit, we dumped their email into a retry queue so that they could be sent at a later point.

We assumed—wrongly as it turned out—that customers would go over their quota gradually, as a result of natural traffic growth. Had this been the case, retrying email over time would have made sense. A handful of email messages get delayed, and as those delays become more common, it nudges the customer onto a dedicated provider instead. In reality, customers were much more likely to catapult over the limit with activities that would trigger email to all of their users—hundreds if not thousands of emails all at once.

That created a situation where the retry queue would fill up to the point where 20 workers would need hours of processing just to clear the messages. It affected the performance of the service for everyone and set off a page to whoever was on call—all over a bunch of email that most of the time no one actually wanted delivered in the first place.

We decided to change the way rate-limiting worked so that instead of retrying email, the shared provider would drop them when the limit was exhausted. That was a lot of migration work, and not only did we have to change the rate-limiting algorithm, but we also had to change the technology that was doing the rate-limiting in the first place. Our existing rate-limiting solution was in the process of being replaced by another solution. We needed to change our architecture and then figure out a backward-compatible strategy for our on-premises customers who upgraded at a slower cadence than cloud customers.

All of this was a lot of work, and our motivation for investing in it was very personal: when the retry queue filled up, it paged someone on our team to go fix it. This was both annoying and disruptive. The interruption was made doubly frustrating by the fact that the official resolution to this issue in our playbook was to drop all the email in the retry queue anyway. It seemed pointless to ask a human to wake up at 3 AM to do what a computer should be able to do automatically.

What we didn't think about until we were in the middle of the change is how much money not trying to send hundreds of thousands of pointless emails was going to save us. We got a certain number of email messages per month from the company that ran the shared email server for us. When we went over that limit, our account with this provider automatically bought 50,000 more emails for $20 and sent us an alert letting us know it had done so. When we started rolling out this change, we were receiving about 10 such alerts a day, or $200 in additional email. A single incident might cost us anywhere from $1,000 to $2,000.

When the changes went live, we literally saved the organization tens of thousands of dollars just by getting rid of email that our customers didn't want sent in the first place. The whole project had been a huge win, but the cost savings gave us political capital that we could spend both to justify why we hadn't spent that time adding new features and to get buy-in for similar maintenance work later.

It can be tricky getting started with opportunity costs because the number of potential opportunities to calculate can seem infinite. Remember that opportunity costs are thought experiments and rhetorical devices. You don't need to list the costs of everything your team might be doing, just the activities that strengthen the case for what you want to be doing. This means highlighting how activities with high prioritization might be more expensive than the organization is assuming and describing in business-friendly language how much value there is to be gained by doing things the way you'd like them to be done.

When looking for the right opportunities to compare against, consider activities from these three general categories.

The Cost of Not Adding New Features

This cost typically is calculated by estimating profits or impact of new features. It is larger in small organizations where the development team may not be big enough to have broken out into distinct units. Shipping a new feature with a small organization locks up a greater percentage of the total staff, which means they are not available to do modernization work or contribute to other projects.

The pressure to delay maintenance work on legacy systems in favor of new features and products is constant at most organizations. There's never a good time for it, although it always seems that if the organization could just get through the latest challenge, things will calm down and the cleanup can begin. To avoid endless procrastination, try to align the new features with the goal state. For example, if migrating from a monolith to services, you might want to use the new feature to identify the first service to peel off.

The Cost of Not Fixing Something Else

Legacy systems rarely have only one thing wrong with them. Each step in the modernization process is a decision between problems that could be fixed with the same time and energy. I've already described various methods for choosing what to fix and when. Opportunity costs are really about selling the strategy up the chain of command. Doing this is easier if the organization has defined *service-level objectives (SLOs)* or has *service-level agreements (SLAs)*. Both SLOs and SLAs equate performance levels with consumer value. SLAs may go as far as defining a specific monetary amount the customer can be reimbursed when performance dips below a specific level.

SLOs and SLAs help the team prioritize fixes by how much pain the problem is causing for users. They are a good thing to have even if you feel confident that you won't need to justify what you modernize and when. But if you do have to justify your strategy, you should be able to study historical data and project under what conditions a given system or part of a system might violate its SLO. Often this is heavily influenced by scale, so it's a good opportunity to leverage the business side's ambition to your advantage: look at what level of growth the business is expecting and calculate opportunity costs based on how that level of growth will affect SLOs.

The Cost of Not Deprecating in Favor of a Different Solution

This is a particularly difficult cost to calculate because deprecations do not complete all at once. For a period of time during a migration or modernization, it's likely that an organization will be maintaining both the old solution and the modern one, especially if the new solution requires code changes to be deployed. So, in addition to the cost of either purchasing or developing the new solution, you have to factor in the cost of decommissioning the old solution. How many teams does that affect? What are they not working on while they make those changes? What is the long-term maintenance burden of the old solution versus the new one? Depending on whether the new solution is hosted/software as a service (SaaS) or just a new custom-built tool, the considerations could look very different.

COMING IN MIDSTREAM

S o far, this book has been operating under the assumption that you are *initiating* the modernization effort at your organization. We've considered strategy that assumes you're on-site to do the planning in the first place. The organization might have attempted to modernize before you were employed there, but I've assumed that the current modernization effort is something you started. However, most modernization efforts I've been involved with in my career have not looked like this. Organizations tend to underestimate the amount of work and level of investment modernization requires. An unfortunate consequence of that assumption is that they do not seek out expertise until they are in trouble.

In my career, the number of modernization efforts I have kicked off is dwarfed by the number of modernization efforts I have parachuted into. I would love to have the luxury of participating in the planning and assessment phases, but rarely do technical leaders think that is necessary.

This chapter describes what to do when you're coming in midstream and the project is already in trouble. Activities can get messy when you're attempting to change legacy systems, and this chapter is full of emergency "break glass here" techniques for untangling the mess.

When a project takes months or years of sustained commitment, no shortage of things can go wrong. In Chapter 3, I mentioned that most modernization stories begin with failure. Coming in when plans are already in motion and not going well limits your options. Pushing the reset button and going back to the drawing board may do more harm than good. A combat medic's first job is to stop the bleeding, not order a bunch of X-rays and put together a diet and exercise plan. To be effective when you're coming into a project that has already started, your role needs to adapt. First you need to stop the bleeding, and then you can do your analysis and long-term planning.

Finding the Bleed

Of course, technology projects do not literally bleed; therefore, identifying the most urgent issues can be a challenge. In this chapter, we discuss the situations I have seen the most often, but I want us to start with some general guidance first.

Find responsibility gaps. There will always be a disconnect between responsibilities formally delegated and actual responsibilities or functionality. Conway's law tells us that the technical architecture and the organization's structure are general equivalents, but no system is a one-to-one mapping of its organization. There are parts of the system with shared ownership, parts that no one is responsible for at all, parts where responsibilities are split in unintuitive ways. When looking for bad technology, debt, or security issues, the most productive places to mine are gaps between what two components of the same organization officially own.

Organizations tend to have responsibility gaps in the following areas:

- So-called 20 percent projects, or tools and services built (usually by a single engineer) as a side project.

- Interfaces. Not so much visual design but common components that were built to standardize experience or style before the organization was large enough to run a team to maintain them.

- New specializations. Is the role of a data engineer closer to a database administrator or a data scientist?

- Product engineering versus whatever the product runs on. DevOps/site reliability engineering (SRE) didn't solve that problem; this just moved it under more abstraction layers. If you've automated your infrastructure configuration, great—who maintains the automation tools?

When there's a responsibility gap, the organization has a blind spot. Debt collects, vulnerabilities go unpatched, and institutional knowledge is gradually lost.

Study the cadence, topics, and invite lists of meetings. Too often, meetings are maladapted attempts to solve problems. So if you want to know what parts of the project are suffering the most, pay attention to what the team is having meetings about, how often meetings are held, and who is being dragged into those meetings. In particular, look for meetings with long invite lists. Large meetings are less effective than small meetings, but they do convincingly spread the blame around by giving everyone the impression that all parties were consulted and all opinions were explored. Meetings with ever-expanding invite lists suggest something is wrong in that area of the project.

Other red flags around meetings include teams that are having planning sessions longer than an hour and teams where check-in meetings are scheduled with less than 48 hours' notice.

Pay attention to the rhetoric of career-minded leaders. It's harsh to say it, but people react to a struggling project in basically two ways. There are the people who roll up their sleeves and focus on helping, even if helping means unglamorous work not usually part of their responsibilities, and then there are the people who spend the time they could be helping drafting excuses that explain why the failure is not their fault. Large, messy, in-progress projects will likely have a mix of both people; look for the second type. The problems they are running away from tend to be the messiest ones.

Look for compounding problems. Coming in midstream means the project hasn't officially failed yet, and what people are getting wrong, they are probably doubling and tripling down on. Projects are rarely doomed by one critical error. It's far more likely that the organization was drowning in dysfunctional structures for months leading up to the failure.

All of these examples are places where natural human reactions actively make the problem worse instead of better. Having unclear responsibilities means teams feel like they are asked to pick up the slack for someone else too often. They become self-righteous and start ignoring tasks that aren't part of their jobs as they see it, making the situation worse. Meetings slow down work, which almost always leads to more meetings. Career-minded leaders claim failure was beyond their control, implicitly blaming the team. They make their employees feel unsafe, which encourages them to avoid the problem areas as well.

If a project is failing, you need to earn both the trust and respect of the team already at work to course-correct. The best way to do that is by finding a compounding problem and halting its cycle. If an organization is having too many meetings, cut all of them and gradually reintroduce them one by one. If career-minded leaders are damaging psychological safety, start educating people about blameless postmortems and just culture. Talk to people and observe how the team behaves as a unit. When you can, it is always better to set up someone else for victory rather than solving the problem yourself.

The rest of this chapter describes various in-progress failures I have seen and what we did to pull the project out of a death spiral.

Mess: Fixing Things That Are Not Broken

We've already looked at a number of reasons organizations try to fix things that aren't broken.

- They assume new technology is more advanced than older technology.
- They aspire to artificial consistency.
- They confuse success with quality.
- They optimize past the point of diminishing returns.

The preeminent target of an organization's desire to fix things that are not broken is the monolith. A monolith in the context of software engineering is a tightly coupled application that configures a variety of functions and features so that they run on a single discrete computing resource. Monoliths were a problem that web development invented. Before the internet reached the scale that made distributed computing possible, there was little reason not to design programs to run on one machine. Lately, it seems like no engineer can bear to suffer a monolith to live. Monolith is the ultimate dirty word. Engineers complain about them endlessly. No one ever wants to admit to building one. Every successful large technical organization seems to have at least one conference talk about the heroic multiyear campaign it staged to remove a monolith.

But if monoliths are so awful, why do so many organizations end up with them?

The opposite of a monolith is service-oriented architecture. Instead of designing the application to host all its functionality on a single machine, functionality is broken up into services. Ideally, each service has a single goal, and typically each has its own set of computing resources. The application is created by coordinating the interaction of these services.

Building a product from the beginning with a service-oriented architecture is usually a mistake. Because you don't have the proper product/market fit figured out yet, integrations and data contracts become a major pain point. A data contract is an implicit agreement written in code between two services that must communicate with one another. We call it a contract because both sides need to send and receive data in the same format for the communication to work. If the server decides to change what data it's sending and the client is not updated accordingly, communication between the services breaks down.

When a team is pivoting and iterating, when the feedback loop between the customer and team is at its shortest, data contracts get broken all the time. Features get added, removed, or moved around. Assumptions get made and either validated or thrown out. Before organizations find a product market fit, they can pivot in wild and unpredictable ways. For example, YouTube started as a video dating service. Groupon started as a platform for organizing social actions. Slack started as an online multiplayer video game. Slack was actually the second time its founder had started building an online game only to realize that the real product was something completely different. His earlier startup, Flickr, had the same origin story.

In general, the level of abstraction your design has should be inversely proportional to the number of untested assumptions you're making. The more abstractions a given design includes, the more difficult changing APIs without breaking data contracts becomes. The more often you break contracts, the more often a team has to stop new work and redo old work. When the product hasn't even launched yet, forcing teams to redo work over and over again doesn't improve the odds of success.

That's why monoliths are so great during the early stages of a product. They are tightly coupled, but their complexity and level of abstraction are low. When an engineer makes a change that breaks another part of the system, she knows it immediately and has access to the code to fix the problem she caused.

Once again, focus on the balance between complexity and coupling. Complex systems have large surface areas. Every process takes more steps, and every part needs its own team to handle its maintenance correctly. The downsides of complexity can be mitigated by running more teams and facilitating communication and knowledge sharing between them. If an organization is able to do that, it can achieve the benefits that can come from making systems more complex. Well-built complex systems often allow for greater customization. They can operate at a larger scale with greater flexibility.

Tightly coupled systems, on the other hand, achieve flexibility by strategically breaking themselves. Every programmer has deployed at least one cheap hack to get around an API or inheritance pattern, usually tacking on a comment that reads "Ugh, do this the right way later." Tightly coupled systems become messy because they accrue debt with each workaround that is deployed. The downsides of tight coupling can be mitigated with engineering standards dictating how to extend, modify, and ultimately play nicely with the coupling. They can also be mitigated by honoring the engineering team's commitment to refactoring on occasion. The benefits of tight coupling are that one person can hold enough knowledge of the system in her head to anticipate behavior in a variety of conditions. The architecture is simpler and, therefore, cheaper and easier to run.

A system has a lifecycle. When it is new, it's often run by a small team and has much more to gain from being tightly coupled than it does from being complex. Small teams building new things frequently throw everything out and start over. Small teams have an easier time honoring engineering standards because there are fewer people to bring to consensus. Even when small teams are at big organizations, they tend to build monoliths because the advantages of a monolith are pretty compelling when you don't know whether what you're building will be successful and need to change things fast, even if your method of changing them is poor. At small organizations, we find people are doing several different jobs at once with roles not so clearly defined. Everyone in the same space is using the same resources. In short, small organizations build monoliths because small organizations *are* monoliths.

Large organizations benefit more from complex systems because they have robust operational units to support them. They have the teams to run and maintain all the moving parts of the system—its platform, its monitoring, and so on. They rarely throw everything out and start over, because they operate at a scale where trying to do that would mean a major migration. Large organizations do well when they transition their monoliths to services, because the problems around communication and knowledge sharing that need to be solved to make complex systems work are problems that large organizations have to solve anyway.

But nobody starts a large organization, just as nobody gives birth to a teenager. They grow up, and as they grow up, the ideal point on the complexity–coupling spectrum shifts. Most monoliths will eventually have to be rethought and redesigned, but trying to pinpoint when is like trying to predict the exact moment you will outgrow a favorite sweater. Some organizations will wait too long, and some will do it too soon. Don't believe anyone who tells you that ditching your monolith is the solution to all your problems. Monoliths can and do scale. Sometimes they are more expensive to scale, but the notion that it is impossible to scale monoliths is false. The issue is that by still having a monolith, you might be giving up benefits that could have a huge impact on operational excellence.

Fixing things that are not broken means you're taking on all the risks of a modernization but will not be able to find the compelling value add and build the momentum that keeps things going. Nontechnical stakeholders will see time and money spent and not understand what the point of it was. This demoralizes engineers and violates trust with the team. Fixing the wrong thing makes it harder to secure the resources to finish and makes it much harder to sell the organization on future modernization efforts that might be more necessary.

Figuring Out Whether Something Needs to Be Fixed

Treating monoliths as inherently bad pushes organizations into fixing them when they're not broken. I had a friend who used to say her greatest honor was hearing a system she built had to be rewritten in order to scale it. This meant she had built something that people loved and found useful to the point where they needed to scale it. Most people in technology do not go into building a system with that expectation. The assumption is that the best way to build something is to build it in such a way that it doesn't need any significant changes for a long time. Optimizing to minimize rewrites might seem like a sensible strategy, but if not properly reined in, it invites behavior that ultimately makes systems more brittle.

Neal Ford, director and software architect at ThoughtWorks, had a saying I'm fond of repeating to engineers on my teams: "Metawork is more interesting than work." Left to their own devices, software engineers will almost invariably over-engineer things to tackle bigger, more complex, long-view problems instead of the problems directly in front of them. For example, engineering teams might take a break from working on an application to write a scaffolding tool for future applications. Rather than writing SQL queries, teams might write their own object relational mapping (ORM). Rather than building a frontend, teams might build a design system with every form component they might ever need perfectly styled.

Decisions motivated by wanting to avoid rewriting code later are usually bad decisions. In general, any decision made to please or impress imagined spectators with the superficial elegance of your approach is a bad one. If you're coming into a project where team members are fixing something that isn't broken, you can be sure they are doing so because they are afraid of the way their product looks to other people. They are ashamed of their working, successful technology, and you have to figure out how to convince them not to be ashamed so that they can focus on fixing things that are actually broken.

Set the expectation that all systems need to be rewritten eventually. Engineers at the highest level write programs that have to be revised. No one is smart enough to anticipate every new use case or feature, every advancement in hardware, or every adjustment or shift that might require code to be rewritten. What works for a large organization might suffocate a small one. Good technologists should focus on what brings the most benefit and highest probability of success to the table at the current moment, with the confidence of knowing they have nothing to prove.

This requires getting consensus from engineering on what it means to be broken in the first place. I've mentioned SLOs/SLAs before, and I will point to them again: define what level of value a system needs to bring to the user. If an ugly piece of code meets its SLO, it might not be broken, it might be just an ugly piece of code. Technology doesn't need to be beautiful or to impress other people to be effective, and all technologists are ultimately in the business of producing effective technology.

But . . . What About Conventions?

Setting the expectation that all code will eventually need to be rewritten does mean that occasionally code needs to be rewritten to bring it in line with modern conventions or to clear debt. The issue of what is worth fixing is full of nuance. When I talk about not fixing things that aren't broken, I'm talking about not breaking up monoliths for the sake of breaking up monoliths and not rewriting code to fit the newest trends for the sake of looking good to outsiders. There are plenty of times when changes needed for long-term performance are hard to justify with existing SLOs alone. Technical debt rarely effects performance in a predictable way. A system could badly need a refactor but look fine on a monitoring dashboard until the day it falls apart all at once. In deciding whether to spend the time and money realigning a system with a given convention, here are some other ways to think about value add other than SLOs:

AGE   The older the convention, the more likely it is to be buried deeply in various parts of a modern stack. Legacy systems that don't conform find that the tools and options available to them get smaller and smaller.

JUSTIFICATION   Why do people who promote this convention promote it? Is it good security practice? Have there been well-documented cases of the convention preventing serious failure?

ADVOCATES   Where is this convention coming from? Is it a big organization many other organizations will have to do business with?

OPENNESS   Is the convention based on or tied to open standards? Are people blocked from adopting this convention by licensing or other proprietary issues?

When Does Breaking Up Add Value?

Since this section has spent a lot of time debunking the suggestion that monoliths are inherently bad and need to be broken up, it makes sense to close it with some advice on when to break up monoliths.

Monoliths can be scaled, but depending on how activity is growing, they may be difficult to scale efficiently. For example, if one part of the system is using more resources than other parts, it makes sense to change to an architecture that allows that piece to be given additional resources while not affecting the other parts of the system.

More often than not, monoliths are broken up because of the way the organization is scaling. If you have hundreds or even thousands of engineers contributing to the same code base, the potential for miscommunication and conflict is almost infinite. Coordinating between teams sharing ownership on the same monolith often pushes organizations back into a traditional release cycle model where one team tests and assembles a set of updates that go to production in a giant package. This slows development down, and more important, it slows down rollbacks that affect the organization's ability to respond to failure.

Breaking up the monolith into services that roughly correspond to what each team owns means that each team can control its own deploys. Development speeds up. Add a layer of complexity in the form of formal, testable API specs, and the system can facilitate communication between those teams by policing how they are allowed to change downstream interactions.

The Compounding Problem: Diminishing Trust

Large, expensive projects kicked off to fix things that are not broken break trust with the nontechnical parts of the organization. It inconveniences colleagues, frustrates them, and sometimes confuses them. A modernization effort needs buy-in beyond engineering to be successful. Spending time and money on changes that will have no visible impact on the business or mission side of operations makes it hard to secure that buy-in in the future.

Unfortunately, software engineers are socialized around the idea that their discipline is so difficult, nonengineers are incapable of understanding even the most basic concepts. Resistance from the nontechnical side of an organization tends to be dismissed as ignorance. That means once trust is violated, a cycle is started. The harder securing buy-in for modernization becomes, the more convinced engineering becomes that the problem is their nontechnical colleagues' intelligence and common sense. Engineering stops even trying to speak to the values and needs of the business side of the organization. The more out-of-touch their proposals become with the organization's needs, the less trust engineering will command.

Solution: Formal Methods

Course-correcting a team that is fixing things that are not broken is a long process. The only thing worse than fixing the wrong thing is leaving an attempt to fix the wrong thing unfinished. Half-finished initiatives create confusing, poorly documented, and harder to maintain systems. If you're coming in early enough that not much has been moved around, by all means, stop the team from doing what it's doing.

Otherwise, you have to stay committed. Your first task has to be getting their initiative to a place where you can stop work without creating a Frankenstein monster. Once you've figured out where that point is, the next challenge is figuring out how to tack on value to the process so that the organization can recover from its mistake stronger.

Monolith breakups and other large-scale redesigns offer an opportunity to change process as well as change code. A silver lining in fixing something that is not broken can be found in treating the fix as an opportunity to experiment with and improve engineering practices. If the organization lacks proper testing, take the opportunity to build out and mature test suites. If the organization doesn't have monitoring, consider what tools might work for the new architecture. If the organization has never done incident response or on-call rotations, use the creation of new services to establish those practices.

If the organization does all of these things already, introduce formal methods.

Formal methods are techniques for applying mathematical checks to software designs to prove their correctness. In attempting to prove correctness, formal methods can highlight bugs that would otherwise be impossible to find just by studying the code. The most accessible form of formal methods is called *formal specification*. It consists of writing out the design as a specification with a markup language that a model checker can parse and run analysis on. These model checkers take the valid inputs defined by the spec and map out every possible combination of output based on the design. Then they compare all those possible outputs to the rules the spec has defined for valid outputs, looking for a result that violates the assertions of the spec.

As of this writing, formal methods are not commonly used by software teams. The learning curve is steep, and resources for beginners are practically nonexistent. The community of users itself is small and skewed slightly toward academia. However, an engineering team doesn't need everyone to know how to write a spec to start using formal methods. An organization can start with just one engineer who works with other teams to draft and refine specs, the same way engineering teams often have a small pool of designers they work with to draft and refine UX.

Formal methods help engineering teams consider a broader array of conditions and scaling factors. They also improve communication between teams by giving everyone a reference detailing the design and expected behaviors of a system.

If you can't find anyone who can make sense of TLA+ syntax or Alloy or Petri nets, one slightly easier way to begin introducing formal methods is with contract testing. *Contract testing* is a form of automated testing that checks whether components of a system have broken their data contracts with one another. When breaking up a monolith into services, honoring these contracts or clearly communicating when they need to be broken is essential to building, integrating, and maintaining a high-performing system. Contract testing is not a form of formal specification per se, but rolling it out follows roughly the same process. It requires every endpoint to have a spec written in a specific markup language that the contract testing tool can parse and check for inconsistencies.

Strongly typed languages sometimes can do contract testing without any additional tools if repositories are set up correctly. For example, if the service owner is responsible for writing the endpoints, the client libraries, and the mocks of the service for testing, they can test for breaking changes on their own.

Mess: Forgotten and Lost Systems

Large organizations lose systems. I don't mean the systems go down; I mean the organizations forget they have them and occasionally lose the records of their existence. Entire product lines are designed to handle this problem: searching for VMs on networks, transversing connections, inspecting dependencies, and managing inventory. It's amazing how common it is, because this seems like something that just shouldn't happen. How can an organization continue to spend money on something it does not know exists?

When an organization is in startup mode, it typically has a small engineering team that handles basically everything. Groups then constantly break off and reform as the architecture is built out. At some point, an organization likely will start to create divisions and delegate ownership, but that's a game of musical chairs that will often leave some parts of the architecture without a seat when the music stops.

Software without maintainers is a key place to find all kinds of monsters, but how do you find what is unowned and forgotten?

One potential approach is to trace the activities of the engineers who were around when things were small. In those early days, strong engineers tend to hop from project to project, applying themselves wherever urgency and interest coincide. Not much thought is likely given to transition planning, because the software is new and would be stable for a while without much in the way of maintenance. If the software is particularly well made, it might slip into obscurity, quietly humming away completely unnoticed because it has never seemed to need maintenance before. Trace the movements of those early engineers as the software was originally being built. What did they touch, and who owns it now?

Another option is to follow the money. Forgotten services still consume resources the organization must pay for. At the least, some record of those transactions should exist. If you're using a commercial cloud provider, start tagging your instances automatically. Doing so will highlight images that are unaccounted for.

The Compounding Problem: Crippling Risk Avoidance

When an architecture is so complex or so old that entire pieces of it are forgotten, engineers can feel as if they are working in a minefield. No one plans effectively for the unknown unless they plan effectively for failure. Without the ability to accept and adapt to failure, the unknown traps individual contributors in a catch-22. Changing a system with unclear boundaries and missing components is likely to trigger an outage. Not taking action increases the odds of failure eventually, but not failure that can be traced to one particular decision or action.

Engineers make decisions that are worse for the health of systems overall but are less likely to trigger outages that they can be blamed for as individuals. Maintaining the system becomes a game of hot potato, with every passing year increasing the risks to greater and greater extremes. Although many of the engineers caught in this trap understand they are choosing the worst possible outcome for everyone, the level of complexity of the system makes it impossible for them ever to feel like they know the system well enough to change it safely.

Solution: Chaos Testing

Ultimately, you must accept that it might not be possible to track down and account for all systems. Even when you find them, figuring out exactly what they do could be difficult. If you're coming into a project with an organization that has forgotten systems, you're probably dealing with a team that is paralyzed by this reality. The engineers might have gotten stuck in the planning phase as they try fruitlessly to figure out whether the latest inventory is correct. They are probably scared of deploying any changes at all to any system, for fear of finding another forgotten system that's also a critical dependency.

You have to be comfortable with the unknown. You can do that by emphasizing *resilience* over reliability. Reliability is important, but too many organizations use reliability to aim for perfection, which is the exact opposite of what they should be trying to accomplish. Site reliability engineers typically talk about performance in terms of number of nines—that is, whether a service is up and running 99.9 percent of the time (three nines), 99.99 percent of the time (four nines), or 99.999 percent of the time (five nines). Since these numbers are calculated as part of SLAs and since SLAs are written into the contract between the organization and its customer, nontechnical people in the organization tend to misunderstand the value of the number of nines. More nines are not always better.

Five nines means a service has fewer than 5.25 minutes of downtime per year. So if something goes wrong, an engineer has only a few minutes to wake up, log on, diagnose, and fix it. And even if she is capable of pulling that off, failure can happen only once a year. A former colleague of mine and an experienced engineer from Google used to like to say, "Anything over four nines is basically a lie." The more nines you are trying to guarantee, the more risk-averse engineering teams will become, and the more they will avoid necessary improvements. Remember, to get five nines or more, they have only seconds to respond to incidents. That's a lot of pressure.

SLAs/SLOs are valuable because they give people a budget for failure. When organizations stop aiming for perfection and accept that all systems will occasionally fail, they stop letting their technology rot for fear of change and invest in responding faster to failure. That's the idea anyway. Some organizations can't be talked out of wanting five or even six nines of availability. In those cases, *mean time to recovery (MTTR)* is a more useful statistic to push than reliability. MTTR tracks how long it takes the organization to recover from failure.

When we encountered systems that had been forgotten and we couldn't figure out what they were doing, we would usually just turn them off and see what happened. For an older generation of technologists, this seems reckless, but modern-day engineering teams refer to this practice as *chaos testing*. Resilience in engineering is all about recovering stronger from failure. That means better monitoring, better documentation, and better processes for restoring services, but you can't improve any of that if you don't occasionally fail.

The rationale around provoking failure deliberately is that if something unexpected does happen, it happens when everyone is on high alert and at a time the organization scheduled specifically for that purpose. When we turned off a system, we waited for someone to complain. That person was either the system owner or the owner of a downstream dependency, but either way, we ended the experiment with more information about what the system was doing than we started with.

If no one complained, we tended just to leave the system off and move on. Having one less component to modernize was still a win. Do we sometimes find out months later that the system we turned off was in fact doing something essential? I won't lie; it does occasionally happen, but that's why investing in testing and monitoring is so important for systems at scale of any age. If something is important enough to build a component specifically to do it, there should be some way of alerting system owners when it doesn't happen.

Mess: Institutional Failures

If a bad pattern is used in one part of a system, it's everywhere in the system. Sometimes an organization doesn't know that string concatenation on database queries is a bad idea (for example). More likely, the bad pattern you're seeing is a result of shifting norms around technical best practices. Remember the days when Facebook thought HTTPS could be optional? What would have been secure practice a few years ago is already riddled with easily exploitable holes.

It stands to reason, therefore, that if you have a piece of software no one has put much thought into maintaining for a few years, there are going to be problems, and those problems are going to be systemic. They will be patterns repeated throughout the system. What reason would the engineering team have to do things differently?

Lately, I've been seeing this kind of rot taking hold within months, rather than years. Particularly on security issues, the turnaround between secure and cracked seems to grow shorter and shorter all the time. If no one has touched something in six months, that is a good place to start the search for problems.

Once you've found a problem, the next step is to determine whether it's a pattern or just a mistake. Security vulnerabilities from out-of-date dependencies are obviously not a pattern. Accidentally removing something that was once in the code is not a pattern. Not escaping inputs, storing secrets in plaintext, returning more information than the requester needs—those are patterns.

Code-checking software can sometimes be useful in tracking down all the instances of a bad pattern. But some problems do not reveal themselves easily and require actual human beings. If you've found such a problem, the first thing to do is define the context around the code. What is it doing? What type of requests trigger it, and what processes and services does it call? The nice thing about patterns is that if you know their context, you can predict them. If a piece of bad code calls a database, the natural place to look for other pieces of bad code is other places that call that database.

In the worst-case scenario, the problems cross application boundaries. Part of analyzing the context of a bad pattern should be its providence. In other words, who built this thing? If the same team built two applications at about the same time, it's unlikely completely different development practices were used.

The Compounding Problem: No Owners

The trouble with systemic issues, whether they're in the code base or the culture, is that no one actually owns them. If they affect everyone and everyone participates in them, the only people with the authority to fix them are the people the least equipped to do so. A CEO or cabinet secretary isn't going to have much luck neglecting their responsibilities in order to dig into implementation issues of one system, no matter how large or critical. Such a leader could delegate the responsibility to a more tactical subordinate, but that appointee would likely find themselves fighting endless political battles.

Problems that impact multiple organizational units require coordination across those boundaries to fix. The more importance an organization gives those boundaries—building budgets and hiring cycles around them—the more people at the top of those units will police their boundaries. This sets up political battles that are often self-reinforcing. Leaders have their fiefdoms. They fought hard for the resources they have. If they reroute even a small portion of those resources to institutional problems while their peers ignore the problem and the problem is not solved, those resources could be permanently forfeited. When there is no precedent for cross-functional collaboration, who will take on the risk of being the first mover?

Solution: Code Yellow

Systemic problems almost always appear midstream. When we find them, I like to document these issues for the wider organization as *BOLOs* (for *be on the lookouts*). We send out a short announcement explaining the problem in plain English, pointing to specific examples we have found and establishing a point of contact on our team for other teams to reach out to if they find similar issues. If the problem is particularly serious, we will set up short talks about the issue, demonstrating what the bad code looks like, how to recognize it, and describe appropriate and inappropriate fixes. Sometimes we reach out to other teams specifically.

Broadly, these techniques are part of a methodology called *Code Yellow*, which is a cross-functional team created to tackle an issue critical to operational excellence. The term *Code Yellow* refers both to the team and the process that governs the team's activities. This was a practice developed at Google to handle issues that were beyond the scope of what any one part of the organization owned. And unlike other processes at Google, it didn't end up documented and commented on in a thousand different management books, so the only people who seem to know what a Code Yellow is or how to run one are former Google people or individuals trained by former Google people. It has spread to other engineering organizations through oral tradition in that way.

The purpose of a Code Yellow is to create momentum. When a legacy system has performance, stability, or security issues that are both systemic and entangled with other issues, it can be overwhelming and demoralizing. Nobody makes things better, because everybody becomes distracted by the total volume of problems. No single improvement feels like it will make enough of an impact to turn the tide.

Code Yellows have the following critical features that ensure their success over other project management approaches:

The Code Yellow leader has escalated privileges. The leader gets to commandeer any and all resources needed for the Code Yellow effort. This includes people, conference rooms, offices, and so on. The leaders can pull these resources off of other teams without approval from the normal chain of command and without lengthy explanation or discussion.

The leader serves as a central point of contact for the effort. Code Yellow issues are often both systemic and sensitive in nature. The organization may not know the full scope of the issue when declaring the Code Yellow. By creating a central point of contact, teams across the organization can refer issues to the Code Yellow leader and receive clear and specific guidance. Unrelated issues can be diagnosed and dispatched easily.

The team is small. Team composition may change as the leader pulls in experts from other teams and releases them, but the size of the team at any one point in time stays less than eight people. Those people should be able to implement solutions; they are not simply representatives from other teams.

The team is focused. When assigned to a Code Yellow, team members are relieved of all other roles and responsibilities so they can focus their energies 100 percent on the Code Yellow.

The Code Yellow is temporary. Before declaring a Code Yellow, the organization should set success criteria. At what level of improvement is the situation no longer critical and the remaining work can be placed on the road maps of existing teams with proper prioritization? Code Yellows can last for months, but they should not run for quarters. The temporary nature of a Code Yellow is what helps conquer the political rivalries that otherwise make systemic problems harder to solve. A Code Yellow guarantees that only resources that are urgently needed will be commandeered and that they will be returned as soon as the crisis is over.

An issue warrants a Code Yellow if it is urgent and the scope is beyond what one cohesive unit of an organization can handle. That usually means a security or a system reliability problem. Occasionally Code Yellows can be used for more nuanced issues that affect the organization's overall competitiveness. In 2008, Google called a Code Yellow after internal studies demonstrated how latency negatively affected users' long-term behaviors:

> One might think that the minuscule amounts of latency involved in the experiment would be negligible—they ranged between 100 and 400 milliseconds. But even those tiny hiccups in delivering search results acted as a deterrent to future searches. The reduction in the number of searches was small but significant, and were measurable even with 100 milliseconds (one-tenth of a second) latency. What's more, even after the delays were removed, the people exposed to the slower results would take a long time to resume their previous level of searching.
>
> [...]

This Code Yellow kicked off at a TGIF where Hölzle metered the performance of various Google products around the world, with a running ticker on the big screen in Charlie's Café pinpointing the deficiencies. "You could hear a pin drop in the room when people were watching how stunningly slow things were, like Gmail in India," says Gabriel Stricker, a Google PR director.[1]

In 2010, another Code Yellow was called to deal with the aftermath of Operation Aurora, a Chinese government cyberattack that rooted Google's corporate network and allowed Chinese intelligence to steal information.

In 2015, the Chromium team (the open source project that backs Google Chrome) called a Developer Productivity Code Yellow to improve performance so that it would be easier to attract and retain contributors.

All of these are critical issues, but they all look different. They have different scopes. Only one presented itself as a traditional crisis. But in each case, the problem would have been difficult for a single team or solitary division to solve. By building a small, empowered team to start off the response, Google was able to create focus and momentum that made impossible problems seem solvable.

Code Yellows end when the issue is out of the critical stage, not when the problem is fully resolved. Part of the Code Yellow should be developing a plan for executing on long-term improvements, upgrades, and development work. How is post–Code Yellow work assigned? Who holds people accountable? The composition of the Code Yellow team should reflect this; if the long-term work will involve specific teams, members of those teams should be part of the Code Yellow. At the end of the Code Yellow, those members return to their teams and continue the Code Yellow work as part of their regular road maps.

---

[1]   Steven Levy, *In the Plex: How Google Thinks, Works, and Shapes Our Lives* (New York: Simon & Schuster, 2011).

It's worthwhile for leadership to have a high tolerance for risk when defining the line of criticality. Code Yellows become less effective the longer and less urgent the work becomes. Having a good plan of how the work will be completed once normal status is restored and holding people accountable produces a better outcome than depending on a small elite team to save you.

Calling a Code Yellow

Code Yellows are declared by the lowest-level leader, not the highest. They should be declared only by leaders who have authority over all the affected parts of the organization. In a small organization, Code Yellows are usually called by someone very senior, but as the organization grows, this practice becomes inefficient and bureaucratic. By granting the authority to the lowest-level leader with authority over all affected areas, the organization is able to continue to move quickly in response to critical issues.

In other words, if the problem is an engineering issue that spans teams under multiple directors, the person with the authority to call a Code Yellow is the vice president of engineering to whom those directors report. If the issue also involves teams of another VP, the person with the authority is one level up from the VPs.

Sometimes the scope of a Code Yellow changes to affect a larger part of the organization as the team uncovers more details. In that case, it is not customary to relitigate the decision to call the Code Yellow itself, although some adjustments to communication strategy and success criteria may be warranted. Status meetings may be expanded to include leaders from other groups, for example.

Code Yellows are not generally called by engineering managers or directors because the scope of their field of influence should be small enough to manage the problem via other project management strategies. Code Yellows are for systemic problems; a problem that fits entirely within the domain of a single engineering manager without touching or affecting any other group is not systemic.

Running a Code Yellow

The Code Yellow leader plays a similar role to that of an incident commander, assigning tasks to team members and serving as the final decision-maker. They need to have enough technical knowledge and implementation experience to do so with confidence. They also need to be able to devote 100 percent of their attention to the Code Yellow. For these reasons, senior leaders are usually a poor choice to run a Code Yellow. Clearing their calendars to focus on a Code Yellow blocks other important things in the organization. They might not understand how the product or architecture works with the detail necessary to make quick decisions. However, the leader need not necessarily be from engineering. Product managers can make excellent Code Yellow leaders, as can staff engineers and principal engineers.

Ideally, the Code Yellow leader should have enough experience with the organization to know who the experts are, which teams own which parts of the product, and so on and so forth. This allows them to keep the team small and limit the amount of discussion around identifying resources.

When declaring a Code Yellow, it's important that the wider organization be made aware of it. If the organization is large, it may not be necessary to broadcast an announcement about the Code Yellow to all employees, but every team that might have relevant information or resources that will be reassigned in the Code Yellow needs to know. This helps smooth the path for the leader when he or she approaches other teams.

Because Code Yellows tend to be sensitive, it's not necessary to provide a great deal of detail in the announcement. If the Code Yellow was triggered by issues, tickets, or discussions that are accessible to everyone, the announcement should link to those internal conversations for reference. Otherwise, the Code Yellow announcement can just define the scope as it is known at the time (for example, "We're declaring a Code Yellow on application security").

The Code Yellow announcement must clearly identify who the leader is, generally with a statement like "John Doe may reach out to you about this."

Part of the leader's responsibility during a Code Yellow is handling communication about the Code Yellow, which includes keeping leadership briefed on progress. Although Code Yellows can be stressful, the more time the leader spends in status update meetings with senior leadership about the Code Yellow, the less time that person spends working on resolving the Code Yellow.

Daily 5- to 15-minute standup calls strike a happy medium but are not required. Some organizations will create either a physical or remote "war room" where the Code Yellow team members operate. If the organization's monitoring tools are robust enough to handle it without significant engineering effort, setting up dashboards to track key metrics around the Code Yellow can help keep everyone focused.

Mess: Leadership Has Lost the Room

Losing the room is a sports term. It means a coach has lost the respect of his or her players. The team, instead of following orders and working together, struggles to self-organize.

This book spends a lot of time discussing value and momentum because success with legacy modernization is less about technical implementation and more about the morale of the team doing the modernizing. So, what can you do if the team you're taking over is so demoralized they won't listen to you long enough to exercise other techniques presented in this book?

People are often too quick to equate morale issues with character flaws. Incentives play a much larger role in who's effective at an organization than some fanciful notion of their character. Organizations that refuse to take responsibility for the situations in which they put their own employees struggle to achieve operational excellence. They discover they possess a unique ability to find and hire the few bad apples in a pool of hundreds of candidates. They watch talent with options walk away and complain about the lack of loyalty, integrity, or mental toughness.

Remember, no one wants to suck at their job. Popular culture sells the myth about lazy, stupid, uncaring bureaucrats. It's easy to dismiss people that way. Buying into the idea that those kinds of problems are really character flaws means you don't have to recognize that you've created an environment where people feel trapped. They are caught between conflicting incentives with no way to win.

An organization doesn't have to be part of the government to be a bureaucracy. When a leader has lost the room, it is usually because the organization has pushed the engineering team back into a place where it is not possible to succeed. It's important not to lose sight of the element of bad faith in this outcome. Teams don't reject their leaders because a project fails or even because a project fails multiple times. Teams reject their leaders when they feel that success was snatched from them. Either they made a real contribution that was ignored or credited to someone else, or their efforts to achieve operational excellence were sabotaged by the leadership in the organization.

Sometimes you can restore trust and bring a team back from the dead just by changing the scenery. Remove old leaders when teams lose faith in them and replace them with new leaders who will gain their trust rather than assume they have it.

But the longer a situation of bad faith is allowed to continue, the deeper the psychological roots grow. The lack of trust in an organization and its leadership can diminish the trust a team has in themselves. Being betrayed by your own leadership is traumatic. One of the ways people process that trauma is by wondering if they deserved it. Removing rejected leaders might solve superficial problems, but it doesn't restore teams back to excellence.

People without confidence self-sabotage. They create self-fulfilling prophecies and display signs of learned helplessness. For example, I had a team once that experienced a high rate of failed deploys, triggering some problem in production at least once a week that required a rollback. The organization had also been leaning on them to produce more and more while cutting their staff and restricting their resources. I took over that team after their old manager was fired, and it was obvious from our first few conversations that the problem wasn't their engineering skills. They had been asked to improve a piece of legacy technology that had not been updated in a while. It had almost no testing, no monitoring, and a complex deploy process.

The reason the legacy system had not been updated in a while was because the organization had been regularly refusing requests to staff a team for the task or invest anything significant in resources. To top it off, the whole infrastructure for this system that processed millions of transactions had been maintained for years by one person.

The team members were completely demoralized. They had lost faith in their ability to ship code safely, so they backed off larger, more creative solutions to technical challenges that might have helped them. They became resigned to their situation, as if outages were inevitable.

They didn't test things. When things went wrong, they didn't do a thorough investigation and confirm what the failure points had been. They avoided those things not because they didn't understand that they were important, but because they had lost faith in their own abilities. After so many failures and years of denied resource requests, they felt other people in the organization assumed they were bad engineers and were desperate to avoid confirming that.

That scenario might sound counterintuitive. If they were so scared of failing, they should have tested more, investigated deeper. Why would they stick with a process that they knew was bad and would increase their likelihood of failure? Like Schrödinger's cat, if they don't have a proper process, they could be both alive and dead at the same time. If they don't have a proper process, they never have to confront the potential reality that they are just bad engineers. It is always possible that a better process would fix all their problems.

However, if they implemented a better process and still failed anyway, they would lose this mental lifeline they were hanging on to. The team doomed itself to failure because they were afraid of learning that the problem the whole time was them—not their process, not the organization's denial of resources, not the inexperienced manager.

The Compounding Problem: Self-Sabotaging Teams

Confidence comes before success. Success rarely creates confidence. When teams don't have confidence in themselves, they will always find something to debunk successful outcomes. They got lucky. The outcome wasn't as good as it should have been or could have been had another team been in charge. The successful outcome did not outweigh past failures.

When people can't accept successful outcomes, they tend to avoid success completely. They self-sabotage because the status quo is safe.

Confidence problems are always compounding. The only thing that convinces people to stop belittling themselves is knowing they have the trust and acceptance of their peers.

Solution: Murder Boards

A murder board is a technique I picked up in government and repurposed for engineering teams. In government, we used them to prep people for Congressional testimony or confirmation hearings, but applying them to a technical challenge was not completely unheard of. NASA's Ames Research Center uses them for satellite launches and requesting funding for research.

The way a murder board works is you put together a panel of experts who will ask questions, challenge assumptions, and attempt to poke holes in a plan or proposal put in front of them by the person or group the murder board exercise is intended to benefit. It's called a murder board because it's supposed to be combative. The experts aren't just trying to point out flaws in the proposal; they are trying to outright *murder* the ideas.

Murder boards are one of those techniques that are really appropriate only in specific circumstances. To be a productive and beneficial exercise, it is essential that the murder board precedes an extremely stressful event. Murder boards have two goals. The first is to prepare candidates for a stressful event by making sure they have an answer for every question, a response to every concern, and mitigation strategy for every foreseeable problem. The second goal of a murder board is to build candidates' confidence. If they go into the stressful event knowing that they survived the murder board process, they will know that every aspect of their plan or testimony has been battle-tested.

I scheduled a murder board for my team with the bad process because I understood that before anything else could get better, the team members needed to learn that their colleagues in engineering did not look down on them. They needed to see that everyone wanted them to succeed, that their past experience of having goal posts moved, resources promised and then taken away, and actions taken in bad faith was over.

They also needed to overcome their fear that they weren't good enough to improve their process or that an improved process wouldn't affect their odds of success. I asked them to write out their plan to test, deploy, and monitor one key upcoming change and be prepared to defend it. They were not thrilled by the idea of doing a murder board. It took me a while to persuade them the exercise could be good. Part of the reason they worried was they felt this exercise would invite colleagues to micromanage them, talk down to them, or treat them like they were stupid and could not be trusted.

I argued that this was an opportunity to prove to everyone how difficult their engineering challenge was. They would leave the murder board with a new process. If the new process still failed, everyone would know it was vetted by the best engineers at the organization and that they couldn't have done any better. In this way, I used the murder board to resolve their fear of opening Schrödinger's box. Failure under a better process would not prove they were bad engineers. That process had survived the murder board and still failed.

To accomplish those goals, it is essential that both sides of the murder board know that the purpose of the exercise is to make the candidate stronger. There must not be any doubt that everyone is on the same team, working for the candidate's benefit. Criticism should be tough, nitpicky, and unforgiving but delivered only if it is relevant to the stressful event to come—in this case, a deploy. For that reason, we don't do murder boards when there is no upcoming stressful event to ground them.

It is useful to set some boundaries with the board. We do not use the murder board space to dredge up old failures or grudges. We do not use the murder board space to put people down or insult them. We don't use it to make grand speeches. The board can ask questions, point out flaws, or provide hypothetical situations. They can provide detailed explanations to elaborate fully on a problem they want to highlight, but they should avoid doing so and let team members speak in their own words as much as possible. Most important, the board's commentary should be exclusively *negative*, even if there are strong advantages to the plan being presented. Murder boards build confidence because they are *survived*.

Stopping the Bleed

The techniques discussed in this chapter are all about transitioning troubled projects to a state where problems are not compounding in cycles. If the organization is making changes that will not provide enough value to justify their expense, boost the value of those changes by turning them into a vehicle of better engineering practices. If the organization is paralyzed by missing information and unknown complications, promote resilience and eliminate the fear of failure. If problems extend beyond what any one team can solve by itself, allow the organization to temporarily reorganize itself around the problem. If teams are demoralized to the point where they are hurting themselves, challenge other parts of the organization to contribute to their success.

Legacy modernization projects do not fail because one mistake was made or something went wrong once. They fail because the organization deploys solutions that actually reinforce unsuccessful conditions. If you're coming into a project in the middle, your most important task as a leader is figuring out where those cycles are and stopping them.

DESIGN AS DESTINY

D esign is not about making things look pretty.

Many software engineers I've worked with have never considered this fact before it was pointed out to them. It's an easy mistake to
make. The most noticeable output of design thinking is packaging—how
we speak about things, how something looks, what features go where,
and how features behave. When we consider the end results, designers
seem most effective when relegated to polishing up a product in the final
stages. We do ourselves and our teams a disservice when we dismiss the
toolkit of a designer in this way. Design is critical to making good technical decisions. *The US Army/Marine Corps Counterinsurgency Field Manual*[1]
put it best when it advised soldiers:

"Planning is problem solving, while design is problem setting."

[1] *The U.S. Army/Marine Corps Counterinsurgency Field Manual* (Chicago: University of Chicago Press, 2007).

Problem-*solving* versus problem-*setting* is the difference between being *reactive* and being *responsive*. Reactive teams jump around aimlessly. Setbacks whittle away their confidence and their ability to coordinate. Momentum is hard to maintain. Responsive teams, on the other hand, are calmer and more thoughtful. They're able to sort new information as it becomes available into different scopes and contexts. They're able to change approaches without affecting their confidence, because design thinking gives them insight into why the change happened in the first place.

With any large, complex project, odds of success are improved if a team can frame the problem and adjust to new information. When done well, problem-setting frees up all members of the team to act autonomously, using their intuition and judgment. At a minimum, problem-setting keeps everybody on the same page about the project's goals and what success looks like. Legacy projects that maximize the impact of design thinking don't just modernize, they innovate.

If those statements sound familiar, it's because I've already described several design exercises for problem-setting in earlier chapters. In Chapter 2, I discussed how working from familiar interfaces increases the likelihood of technology being adopted. In Chapter 3, I explained how to map a system in terms of complexity and coupling. In Chapter 5, I introduced troubleshooting difficult technical conversations with scoping. All of these were design exercises. Now it's time to dive deeper and explore some variations on the problem setting approaches I've already covered.

The first part of this chapter focuses on applying design techniques to technical decision-making: how to structure technical conversations, scope problems, and come to a consensus.

The second part of this chapter focuses on using design techniques to align incentives. In the previous chapter, I mentioned how conflicting incentives can doom projects and demoralize teams; this chapter describes how to figure out what the incentives are within the organization and how to position teams for success given that information.

Designing Technical Conversations

Chapter 5 introduced the concept of scope as a solution to avoid unproductive meetings, but in reality, the process of managing a major modernization is all about manipulating scope.

Scope is determined by what problem you want solve, but few problems exist completely independent from other factors. Deciding which factors actually have influence over the success or failure of that marquee problem and which do not requires thorough and regular feedback. You will have to become adept at collecting data because the factors that can complicate a modernization project are many. They include the historical context, the technical constraints, the skills available through human capital, and internal politics.

On top of that, some of the information delivered to you by those feedback loops will be incorrect, or you will interpret them incorrectly. The simplest form of design exercise is to talk to your user. Doing that is better than doing nothing, but in unstructured conversations, the quality of the feedback can vary. Sometimes users don't know what they want. Sometimes the user and the researcher use the same words to mean different things. Sometimes the power dynamics between the user and the person conducting the interview are so great, the user tells the interviewer what he or she wants to hear.

Design thinking changes the way we address that challenge. It highlights how we ask, who we ask, and who does the asking as determining factors in what information comes to the surface and gets discussed in the first place.

Don't underestimate the role social dynamics have in skewing the accuracy of your information. We know that people behave differently when they are being observed. We know that people tend to be conflict-averse and go along with crowds. We know that not every voice on an engineering team carries the same weight. Design exercises can succeed where normal technical conversations fail because they account for those influences.

If we think of the average technical conversation as being adversarial in nature with individuals either proposing solutions or challenging the ideas of others, team members have plenty of opportunities to engage in unproductive behavior. What makes them look smart in front of the group won't necessarily translate to good technical strategy.

But with design, we can change the path to winning the argument. During a normal team conversation, individual members are looking either to increase or to maintain their status among the group. And, what increases their status? Shooting down the ideas of others. Demonstrating their ability to see some critical flaw everyone else has missed. Developing a brilliant solution. Of those options, developing a brilliant solution is the most difficult to accomplish. Shooting down other people's ideas is usually much easier. So, environments where team members are jockeying for status can overselect for this behavior.

Now, imagine that we started the conversation by telling the team we would give them points for coming up with solutions that used a specific piece of technology. The amount of time spent shooting down ideas would plummet as everyone focused on curating the longest list of potential solutions.

That's the value of design. When we design our conversations, we turn them into games. We redirect the energy of team members into providing more and better answers instead of simply being right and their colleagues wrong.

How to Run a Design Exercise

My goal in including a chapter on design in this book is not to turn software engineers into designers. I'm skeptical of the habit of technical people to assume they can pick up disciplines on the fly that others have spent years cultivating and studying. I believe that technical people should focus on bringing technical expertise to the table and seek out other experts to complement their skills. Therefore, I encourage you to incorporate design thinking into your process by hiring a designer or, even better, consulting the designers you already employ.

That being said, it is useful to understand how design thinking works. Design exercises come in various shapes and sizes, but they share these four distinct phases:

WARM-UP The warm-up creates a break from the distractions of everyday life so that the participants in the exercise are focused on the task at hand. The simplest warm-ups are listing a few sentences introducing your topic/goal/intention, but more active and complicated exercises might devote more time and energy to warming up. Posing a simple question for group discussions, pair work, or polling people for experiences all can be used as warm-ups.

RESEARCH QUESTIONS When we do a design exercise, we do it with a specific research question in mind. We have a problem or a decision to make, and we want to hear other perspectives. Or, we're about to invest in a new product, and we want to know if the users will like it. The most common design exercise for engineering teams is observing potential users interacting with a product. A good researcher will be careful not to lead users, not to teach them how to use the product, but let them interact with it organically and use carefully worded questions to direct them to functions relevant to the research objective.

FOLLOW-UPS People often say things we don't expect in design exercises, requiring us to divert from the structure we've set out for a moment to understand this new piece of information. Follow-up questions or activities are used to go deeper on individual issues as they appear.

AGGREGATION At some point—maybe after a single exercise or after a series of interviews—we need to look at all the data and draw a conclusion. Just like engineering, design is often an iterative process. The conclusion of one exercise may create the research question for the next. For example, if a user research session reveals that users don't understand how to interact with the product, future research sessions will test alternative interfaces until the organization has found something that works for users.

More About Follow-ups: Why vs. How

Creating effective follow-up questions is an art form unto itself. As with research questions, be careful that they don't suggest their own answers or create ambiguities that might bias the data, but unlike with devising research questions, it is nearly impossible to anticipate everything you might want to follow up on ahead of time. You need to write the questions on the fly.

A good rule of thumb is questions that begin with *why* produce more abstract statements, while questions that begin with *how* generate answers that are more specific and actionable. Think about how your answer would be different if the follow-up were "What are the best tools for the job?" versus "How do you know these tools are the best for the job?" You might list a bunch of common solutions in the answer to the first question, convinced that they are good because they are popular. You are more likely to describe your various experiences with the tools you actually use when asked the second question.

Both *why* questions and *how* questions can be useful. *Why* questions broaden the boundaries of the research field by allowing unseen factors and forces to be introduced into the data. *How* questions put you in the minds of users so you can see those factors as they understand them. *Why* questions often lead to *how* questions.

Some Useful Design Exercises for Engineering Teams

Design is a rich industry full of interesting approaches and philosophies, more than what a single chapter can capture. To get you started, I've provided a few of my favorite exercises for technical conversations. Think of this as a toolkit. Some of these exercises are loosely adapted from *The Surprising Power of Liberating Structures: Simple Rules to Unleash a Culture of Innovation* by Henri Lipmanowicz and Keith McCandless, which is a great resource for further learning.[2]

Exercise: Critical Factors[3]

This is a brainstorming exercise to do with a team to help prioritize conversations around the early stages of a modernization activity. What must happen for the project goals to be successful? What must not happen? After everyone has had their say and recorded their ideas, the team edits the list to make sure everything on it really deserves to be there. A good way to do that is for the team to discuss each item in terms of whether the project could succeed if everything else on the list of critical factors went favorably. The only items that should remain on the list are the factors that have the ability to take down the entire project by themselves.

After actions: Early technical conversations should focus on achieving or maintaining good outcomes for these critical factors. In-scope issues move outcomes along these critical factors in a positive direction. Out-of-scope issues do not affect these outcomes.

Exercise: The Saboteur[4]

A similar but inverse brainstorming exercise to the critical factors exercise is asking your team to play saboteur. If you wanted to guarantee that

---

[2] Henri Lipmanowicz and Keith McCandless, *The Surprising Power of Liberating Structures: Simple Rules to Unleash a Culture of Innovation* (Seattle: Liberating Structures Press, 2016).

[3] "Min Specs: Specify Only the Absolute 'Must Dos' and 'Must Not Dos' for Achieving a Purpose," Liberating Structures, accessed February 2020, *http://www.liberating structures.com/14-min-specs/*.

[4] "Making Space with TRIZ: Stop Counterproductive Activities and Behaviors to Make Space for Innovation," Liberating Structures, accessed February 2020, *http://www .liberatingstructures.com/6-making-space-with-triz/*.

the project fails, what would you do? How can you achieve the worst possible outcome? Once this list is generated, the team discusses if there are any behaviors either internally or from external partners that are close to items on the saboteur list.

After actions: Some of the behaviors on the saboteur list will be habits or ineffective processes that need to be changed. Depending on your results, these items might be worth handling as critical factors. More likely, though, the saboteur list will show you where the fault lines are in your team. What distractions are they the most vulnerable to? How well do they understand their true threats? How do internal politics manifest among team members? The saboteur exercise should help you anticipate out-of-scope issues that are likely to be brought up and who they are likely to come from. Having a sense of that from the beginning helps keep technical conversations on track. If you're able to open your meetings by defining what is and is not in scope, it is much easier to hold everyone accountable.

Exercise: Shared Uncertainties[5]

This exercise also starts by asking team members to identify potential risks and challenges to a project's success, but this time, you're looking for differences in how such risks are perceived. Give each team member a four-quadrant map with the following axes:

SIMPLE TO COMPLEX Problems are simple if they are well defined and understood. They are complicated if their causes are unknown or if solving them means giving up something else of value.

ORDERLY TO CHAOTIC Problems are orderly when there isn't much debate about the correct way to solve them, although those solutions

---

5. "Critical Uncertainties: Develop Strategies for Operating in a Range of Plausible Yet Unpredictable Futures," Liberating Structures, accessed February 2020, *http://www .liberatingstructures.com/30-critical-uncertainties/*.

might be long and tedious. They are chaotic when their solutions could accidentally make the situation worse.

Each team member places challenges somewhere on this map. Then as a group they compare results. How far apart are they? Where are the shared anxieties? Is anyone completely out of sync with everyone else? Depending on your team's composition, you might want to agree on the challenges to be mapped in advance or let individuals come up with the challenges to map as a group. The advantage to not getting everyone on the same page before mapping is if your team draws from different organizational units or functions, you can better see knowledge gaps by not requiring them all to use the same challenges.

After actions: By far the biggest benefit of this exercise is that it introduces alternative perspectives and priorities in a way that is not confrontational. In open discussions, different perspectives are often presented as responses to other people sharing their own perspectives. This makes the contribution feel like a counterargument and encourages people not to empathize with or listen to each other.

There's also an inherent sense of prioritization when overlap and consensus are high on the team. If a certain challenge is thought to be orderly and simple by everyone, the team might prefer to consider it out of scope until strategies are developed around harder problems.

Regarding simple/chaotic and orderly/complex problems, if you have any of those, they are good issues to focus early conversations around. They are often the most intimidating and anxiety-inducing.

Exercise: The 15 Percent[6]

In Chapter 3, I talked about the value of making something 5 percent, 10 percent, or 20 percent better. This exercise asks team members to map out how

---

6. "15% Solutions: Discover and Focus on What Each Person Has the Freedom and Resources to Do Now," Liberating Structures, accessed February 2020, *http:// www.liberatingstructures.com/7-15-solutions/*.

much they can do on their own to move the project toward achieving its goals. What are they empowered to do? What blockers do they foresee, and when do they think they become relevant? How far can they go without approval, and who needs to grant that approval when the time comes?

Have each team member brainstorm an ordered list of actions they can take right now to make the situation 15 percent better. The number 15 is arbitrary; don't quibble over whether the impact of actions would really be only an 8 percent improvement. The point is these actions don't need to come close to solving the problem; they just need to move things forward.

When each team member has a list, the team should discuss the items, refine them as needed, and make a commitment to execute.

After actions: The best technical conversations are the ones you don't need to have. This exercise helps teams figure out where they need to make decisions versus where they need only advise and support other team members. Discussing potential blockers and approvers helps focus the invite lists of whatever conversations do need to be scheduled to the most relevant people. Nothing produces out-of-scope digressions more effectively than having people in meetings who don't need to be there.

Exercises Specifically for Decisions

The exercises described previously all assume that once information is collected and exposed to the team, the right decisions are self-evident. It doesn't always work that way. When you've collected all the data as a team and had a good, thorough discussion about it, here are two additional exercises that focus on decision-making.

Exercise: Probabilistic Outcome-Based Decision-Making

Probabilistic outcome-based decision-making is better known as *betting*. It's a great technique for decisions that are hard to undo, have potentially serious impacts, and are vulnerable to confirmation bias. I tend to use it a lot to run hiring committees, for example. Firing people is difficult;

making a wrong hire can destroy a team's productivity, and people often see what they want to see in potential candidates.

This is how it works: as a group, we make a list of potential outcomes from the decision that needs to be made. Outcomes like "We're able to scale 2× by doing this" or "We will implement this new feature by this date." You can mix both positive and negative outcomes if you like, but I find the conversation usually goes better if the list of outcomes is either positive or negative.

Then team members place bets as to whether the outcome will come true. Traditionally, this exercise is run with imaginary money. Depending on the specific decision to be made, I sometimes ask them to bet with hours of their time instead of money.

The mechanics of the bet work the same way they do in any other context. If you bet a lot and win, you gain a lot. If you bet a lot and lose, you lose a lot. Therefore, just asking someone to put a unit value next to an outcome is forcing them to articulate a confidence level. The wondrous thing about this design is that if you ask people to rate their confidence level between 1 and 10, most of them would struggle to answer. It's the unit itself, the knowledge of how much a dollar or an hour means to them, and what it means to lose a certain amount of dollars or time that helps research subjects articulate their feelings. It doesn't matter that they will not lose what they've bet, just imagining *this much money* or *that much time* is enough to help people place where their feelings are on a spectrum.

You can do this exercise alone when struggling with your own decisions. When I do it with teams, I like to put everyone's bets for each outcome in a shared document or on a whiteboard. Then we discuss how confident the team feels that the positive outcomes would be reached by making the decision one way or the other. By this point, the right decision is usually much more obvious.

Exercise: Affinity Mapping

Affinity mapping is a common design exercise involving clustering ideas and statements from individuals together visually. This involves a large empty surface, usually a wall or a whiteboard, and generally some markers and Post-it Notes. You've probably done affinity mapping before. Everyone writes down their thoughts, one per Post-it Note, and puts it on the wall. Meanwhile, a moderator moves the Post-it Notes around, assembling them into groups of common ideas or feelings.

Affinity mapping works well for category building, but it can also reveal the specific circumstances that make reaching a consensus on a particular decision so difficult: Often in open discussions, people will talk past one another or assume they mean the same thing when expressing different concepts. Affinity mapping can reveal how far apart from one another the group really is and where the biggest points of disagreement actually are.

Team Structure, Organization Structure, and Incentives

In 1968, Melvin Conway published a paper titled "How Do Committees Invent?"[7] This paper, originally intended for *Harvard Business Review* but rejected for being too speculative in nature, outlined the ways the structure and incentives of an organization influenced the software product it produced. It received little response but eventually made its way to the chair of the University of North Carolina at Chapel Hill's computer science department, Fred Brooks. At the time, Brooks had been pondering a question from his exit interview at IBM: Why is it so much harder to manage software projects than hardware projects? Conway's insight linking the structure of software to the structure of the committees that invented it seemed significant enough for Brooks to repackage the thesis as "Conway's law" when he published his guide on effectively managing software teams, titled *The Mythical Man-Month*, in 1975.[8]

[7.] Melvin E. Conway, "How Do Committees Invent?," *Datamation*, April 1968, 28–31.

[8.] Frederick Brooks, *The Mythical Man-Month* (Reading, MA: Addison-Wesley, 1995).

Yet, this was not the only useful observation in Conway's paper. As it has subsequently been referenced by hundreds of computer science texts since Brooks's adoption of it as a universal truth, the more nuanced observations that supported Conway's argument have largely been omitted from the conversation. Conway's law has become a voodoo curse—something that people believe only in retrospect. Few engineers attribute their architecture successes to the structures of their organizations, but when a product is malformed, the explanation of Conway's law is easily accepted.

Conway's original paper outlined not just how organizational structure influenced technology but also how human factors contributed to its evolution. Some of his other observations include the following:

- Individual incentives have a role in design choices. People will make design decisions based on how a specific choice—using a shiny new tool or process—will shape their future.

- Minor adjustments and rework are unflattering. They make the organization and its future look uncertain and highlight mistakes. To save face, reorgs and full rewrites become preferable solutions, even though they are more expensive and often less effective.

- An organization's size affects the flexibility and tolerance of its communication structure.

- When a manager's prestige is determined by the number of people reporting up to her and the size of her budget, the manager will be incentivized to subdivide design tasks that in turn will be reflected in the efficiency of the technical design—or as Conway put it: "The greatest single common factor behind many poorly designed systems now in existence has been the availability of a design organization in need of work."

Conway's observations are more important in the maintaining of existing systems than they are in the building of new systems.

Organizations and products both change, but they do not always change at the same pace. Figuring out whether to change the organization or change the design of the technology is just another scaling challenge.

Individual Incentives

How do software engineers get ahead? What does an engineer on one level need to accomplish for an organization to be promoted to another level? Such questions are usually delegated to the world of engineering managers and not incorporated into technical decisions. And yet, the answers absolutely have technical impacts.

Most of us have encountered this in the wild: a service, a library, or a piece of a system that is inexplicably different from the rest of the applications it connects to. Sometimes this is an older component of the system reimplemented using a different set of tools. Sometimes this is a new feature. It's always technology that was trendy at the time the code was introduced.

When an organization has no clear career pathway for software engineers, they grow their careers by building their reputations externally. This means getting drawn into the race of being one of the first to prove the production-scale benefits of a new paradigm, language, or technical product. While it's good for engineering teams to experiment with different approaches as they iterate, introducing and supporting new tools, databases, languages, or infrastructures increases the complexity of maintaining the system over time. One organization I worked for had an entire stable of custom-built solutions for things such as caching, routing, and message handling. Senior management hated this but felt their complaints—even their instructions that it stop—did little to course-correct. Culturally, the engineering organization was flat, with teams formed on an ad hoc basis. Opportunities to work on interesting technical challenges were awarded based on personal relationships, so the organization's regular hack days became critical networking events. Engineering wanted to build difficult and complex solutions to advertise their skills to the lead engineers who were assembling teams.

Stern lectures about the importance of choosing the right technology for the job did not stop this behavior. It stopped when the organization hired engineering managers who developed a career ladder. By defining what the expectations were for every experience level of engineering and hiring managers who would coach and advocate for their engineers, engineers could earn promotions and opportunities without the need to show off.

Organizations end up with patchwork solutions because the tech community rewards explorers. Being among the first with tales of documenting, experimenting, or destroying a piece of technology builds an individual's prestige. Pushing the boundaries of performance by adopting something new and innovative builds it even more so.

Software engineers are incentivized to forego tried and true approaches in favor of new frontiers. Left to their own devices, software engineers will proliferate tools, ignoring feature overlaps for the sake of that one thing tool X does better than tool Y that is relevant only in that specific situation.

Well-integrated, high-functioning software that is easy to understand usually blends in. Simple solutions do not do much to enhance one's personal brand. They are rarely worth talking about. Therefore, when an organization provides no pathway to promotion for software engineers, they are incentivized to make technical decisions that emphasize their individual contribution over integrating well into an existing system.

Typically, this manifests itself in one of three different patterns:

- Creating frameworks, tooling, and other abstraction layers to make code that is unlikely to have more than one use case theoretically "reusable"

- Breaking off functions into new services, particularly middleware

- Introducing new languages or tools to optimize performance for the sake of optimizing performance (in other words, without any need to improve an SLO or existing benchmark)

Essentially, engineers are motivated to create named things. If something can be named, it can have a creator. If the named thing turns out to be popular, the engineer's prestige increases, and her career will advance.

This is not to say that good software engineers should never break off a new service or introduce a new tool or try a new language on a production system. There just needs to be a compelling reason why those actions benefit the system versus benefit the prospects of the individual engineer.

Most of the systems I work on rescuing are not badly built. They are badly maintained. Technical decisions that highlight individuals' unique contributions are not always comprehensible to the rest of the team. For example, switching from language X to language Z may in fact boost memory performance significantly, but if no one else on the team understands the new language well enough to continue developing the code, the gains realized will be whittled away over time by technical debt that no one knows how to fix.

The folly of engineering culture is that we are often ashamed of signing up our organization for a future rewrite by picking the right architecture for right now, but we have no misgivings about producing systems that are difficult for others to understand and therefore impossible to maintain. This was a constant problem for software engineers answering the call to public service from organizations like US Digital Service and 18F. When modernizing a critical government system, when should the team build it using common private sector tools and train the government owners on said tools, and when should the solution be built with the tools the government worker already knew? Wasn't the newest, greatest web application stack always the best option? Conway argued against aspiring for a universally correct architecture. He wrote in 1968, "It is an article of faith among experienced system designers that given any system design, someone someday will find a better one to do the same job. In other words, it is misleading and incorrect to speak of the design for a specific job, unless this is understood in the context of space, time, knowledge, and technology."

Minor Adjustments as Uncertainty

Joel Spolsky once described rewriting software as the single worst strategic mistake any organization could make, but he attributed its nearly universal appeal to a clever maxim that *code is easier to write than read.*[9]

And it's true; code is easier to write than read. Nearly every software engineer has had the experience of pulling up an old project and finding code that she wrote virtually incomprehensible.

But that doesn't explain why we see the same behaviors with infrastructure, data storage, and other products that do not involve writing code.

One of the major themes that influences how systems degrade over time is how terrible human beings are at probability. We tend to overestimate the likelihood of events recurring once we have already seen them and underestimate the likelihood of events that have not yet happened. Sidney Dekker, a professor of human factors and system safety, called the outcome of this cognition problem on system safety *drift.*[10] Systems do not generally fail all at once; they "drift" into failure via feedback loops caused by a desire to prevent failure. Let's suppose a worker is given a set of checklists with necessary steps to maintain the system in good working order. If she misses a step and the system doesn't fail immediately, her perception of risk changes. Skipping that

[9] Joel Spolsky, "Things You Should Never Do, Part I," Joel on Software, April 6, 2000, *https://www.joelonsoftware.com/2000/04/06/things-you-should-never-do-part-i/.*

[10] Sidney Dekker, *Drift into Failure* (Abingdon-on-Thames, UK: Routledge, 2018).

step becomes not such a big deal, unlikely to cause failure. The more she skips the step, the more convinced of the safety of her action she becomes. She overlooks the possibility that she could have just gotten lucky. The more corners she cuts, the more prone to failure the system becomes.

At the same time, if the system fails for a reason not represented in her checklist, she overestimates the odds of such a failure happening again. The system could have failed because there was a significant flaw, or it could have failed because of a random series of events unlikely to recur. Her ability to respond appropriately is determined by her ability to assess the probability of what has just happened correctly. If she overestimates, she will find new steps to add to the checklist to ensure that an unlikely failure does not recur. Over time, the checklists become more and more cumbersome and increase the likelihood that either she or one of her colleagues will skip a step.

The systems we like to rewrite from scratch are usually the systems we have been ignoring. We don't know how likely failure is because we pay attention to them only when they fail and forget about them otherwise. A hundred errors on a legacy system is not failure-prone if it handles two million requests over that period. When looking at legacy systems, we tend to overrepresent failures.

The systems we like to rewrite from scratch also tend to be complex with many layers of abstraction and integrations. When we change something on them, it doesn't always go smoothly, particularly if we've slipped up in our test coverage. The more problems we have making changes, the more we overestimate future failures. The more a system seems brittle, failure-prone, and just impossible to save, the more a full rewrite feels like an easier solution.

Our perception of risk cues up another cognitive bias that makes rewrites more appealing than incremental improvements on a working system: whether we are trying to ensure success or avoid failure. When success seems certain, we gravitate toward more conservative, risk-averse solutions. When failure seems more likely, we switch mentalities completely. We go bold, take more risks.[11]

If we are judging odds correctly, this behavior makes sense. Why not authorize that multimillion-dollar rewrite if the existing system is doomed?

The problem is we're most likely not judging the odds correctly. We're overemphasizing failure that may be rare and underestimating both the time it will take to complete the rewrite and the performance gains of the rewrite itself. We are swapping a system that works and needs to be adjusted for an expensive and difficult migration to something unproven.

It's the minor adjustments to systems that have not been actively developed in a while that create the impression that failure is inevitable and push otherwise rational engineers toward doing rewrites when rewrites are not necessary.

Organization Size and Communication

Every working person has experienced how an organization's size affects its patterns of communication. When small, an organization communicates in an open and fluid manner. It is possible for everyone in the organization to build a relationship with one another. As the organization grows, knowing everyone else becomes less and less feasible. Coordination requires trust. Given a choice, we prefer to base our trust on the character of people we know, but when we scale to a size where that is not possible anymore, we gradually replace social bonds with process. Typically this happens when the organization has reached the size of around 100 to 150 people.

[11.] See the work of Daniel Kahneman and Amos Tversky on the pseudocertainty effect for more detail, as well as their bestseller book *Thinking, Fast and Slow* (New York: Farrar, Straus and Giroux 2011).

One of the benefits of microservices, for example, is that it allows many teams to contribute to the same system independently from one another. Whereas a monolith would require coordination in the form of code reviews—a personal, direct interaction between colleagues—service-oriented architecture scales the same guarantees with process. Engineers document contracts and protocols; automation is applied to ensure that those contracts are not violated, and it prescribes a course of action if they are.

For that reason, engineers who want to "jump ahead" and build something with microservices from the beginning often struggle. The level of complexity and abstraction is out of sync with the communication patterns of the organization.

Manager Incentives

An engineering manager is a strange creature in a technical organization. How should we judge a good one from a bad one? Unfortunately, far too often managers advance in their careers by managing more people. And if the organization isn't properly controlling for that, system design will be overcomplicated by the need to broadcast importance.

Opportunities to go from being an engineering manager to a senior engineering manager come up from time to time as an organization grows and changes. It's the difference between handling one team and handling many. Managers leave, new teams form, and existing teams grow past their ideal sizes. A good manager could easily earn those opportunities in the normal course of business. Going from senior manager to director, though, is more difficult. Going from director to vice president or higher is even more so. It takes a long time for an organization to reach that level of growth organically.

Organizations that are unprepared to grow talent end up with managers who are incentivized to subdivide their teams into more specialized units before there are either enough people or enough work to maintain such a unit. The manager gets to check off the career-building experience of running multiple teams, hiring more engineers, and taking on more ambitious projects, and the needs of the overall architecture are ignored.

Scaling an organization before it needs to be scaled has similar consequences to scaling technology before it needs to be scaled. It restricts your future technical choices. A complex architecture means the organization must successfully anticipate a number of future requirements and determine how code should be best abstracted to create shared services based on those predictions. Rarely are all of those predictions right, but once a shared service is deployed, changing it is difficult.

In the same way, managers sometimes subdivide their team before there is need to do so. When this happens, they are making predictions about future needs that may or may not come true. In my last role, our director of engineering decided the new platform we were building needed a dedicated team to manage data storage. Predictions about future scaling challenges supported her conclusions, but to get the head count for this new team, she had to cut it from teams that were working on the organization's existing scaling challenges. Suddenly, new abstractions around data storage that we didn't need yet were being developed, while systems that affected our SLAs had maintenance and updates deferred.

Carrying existing initiatives to completion was not as attractive of an accomplishment as breaking new ground. But the problem with designing team structure around the desired future state of the technology is if it doesn't come true, the team is thrown into the chaos of a reorganization.

Designing a Team: Applications of Conway's Law

The challenge of applying Conway's law in a proactive and positive manner is that divisions of work on technical projects can shift depending on the technical challenge being addressed.

Let's say we have an organization building a system that is composed of three web services. Each service has its own repository of code, its own machine images, and its own deployment schedule. Each has a three-tier structure: an application layer, a data access layer, and a frontend. In the beginning, the frontend and the application are logically separate but hosted in the same code repository for convenience. The frontend is just HTML and some CSS and JavaScript files.

Our engineering teams probably reflect this structure. For each service, we have a frontend person and some backend people. We want the look and feel of these services to be the same because they are one system, so we have a design org that is separate from the three development teams, but it produces style guides and assets used by all of them. Maybe we assign a specific point of contact on the design team for each engineering team. We do the same thing for our operations and security groups. Their work is overarching and common to all teams, and we want consistent implementation. We don't want each engineering silo to reinvent the wheel.

Now let's say we want to start using a frontend framework like React, Angular, or Vue.js. We still want each service to have the same look and feel, but we also want to minimize duplicate efforts. They should reuse UI components. Who writes that code? Where does that code live? Do we move the frontend engineers out of the product engineering groups and into a separate group like the designers, security engineers, and operations people, or do we keep them where they are and establish a matrix division to handle the shared development work?

The problem with seeing Conway's law as prescriptive is that technology is filled with little shifts in perception like this. The technology in our example has not fundamentally changed, but our groupings of what belongs with what have changed. We could tell the same story in reverse: what if we want to transition away from a traditional operations team to a DevOps model? Do our operations people now get moved to the product engineering teams? Do backend engineers learn the DevOps tools with operations acting as an oversight authority? Do we keep operations where it is and just ask them to automate?

Reorgs Are Traumatic

The reorg is the matching misused tool of the full rewrite. As the software engineer gravitates toward throwing everything out and starting over to project confidence and certainty, so too does the software engineers' manager gravitate toward the reorg to fix all manner of institutional ills.

And like a full rewrite, sometimes this is the appropriate strategy, but it is not nearly the right strategy as often as it is used. Reorgs are incredibly disruptive. They are demoralizing. They send the message to rank and file engineers that something is wrong—they built the wrong thing or the product they built doesn't work or the company is struggling. It increases workplace anxiety and decreases productivity. The fact that reorgs almost always end up with a few odd people out who are subsequently let go exacerbates the issue.

They are also easy to get wrong, creating new silos where information once flowed freely. Organizations are almost always a little behind in capturing and documenting the state of things in flight. Reorgs orphan in-progress initiatives, particularly the ones focused on long-term maintenance, resulting in information loss and follow-ups dropped.

I think of reorgs as major surgery. If something is seriously wrong, it's worthwhile to risk it, but you wouldn't trust a doctor who wanted to open you up because a kidney was just an inch too far to the right. Similarly, you shouldn't hire managers who want to reorg because they read a blog post that said engineering teams work better when structured this particular way or that particular way.

Sometimes an organization doesn't grow in an orderly fashion, and as a result, teams end up owning a combination of things that don't go together or sharing ownership of things that more properly should have one owner. These are the sorts of situations where reorgs make sense.

Conway's law is a tendency, not a commandment. Large, complex organizations can develop fluid and resilient communication pathways; it just requires the right leadership and the right tooling. Reorgs should be undertaken only in situations where an organization's structure is completely and totally out of alignment with its implementation.

Finding the Right Leadership

Modernization projects are ultimately about transitions. You are moving resources, adjusting processes, and reimagining implementation. The teams that make sense in the beginning do not always make sense at the end.

To find the right leadership, look for people who have been successful in a wide variety of different contexts—old systems, new systems, big bureaucracies, and small startups. Do not hire aspirationally. Do not hire people whose only experiences are working in companies that reflect your desired end state. Do not hire based on what you wish were true about your organization. This is a pretty common mistake. Organizations that want to grow big recruit executives from big organizations. Organizations that want to migrate to the cloud recruit executives who supervised cloud products.

Transitions are inherently ambiguous, and the most important characteristic of any leader who steps into a transition is the ability to adapt to the changing conditions that ambiguity opens up. You can assess those skills in interviews, but the best indicator is usually a candidate's career path. Candidates who are good at adapting have experiences of different sizes and industries on their résumés. They might have done nonprofit or government work. They might have dipped their toes into different careers or roles. They might have left the working world for a few years and then successfully come back.

Candidates who have spent seven or eight years essentially in the same type of organization may bring a lot to the table, but they might also be too attached to one way of doing things. They might not understand why certain approaches work in this situation but not that situation. They might be bureaucratic, risk-averse, and not willing to rise to the challenge of a different environment.

Transitions are all about change, but determining *what* should change and *when* it should change are significant questions. We didn't get where we are all at once. Why should we get anywhere else that way? Leaders who are comfortable with ambiguity have a higher likelihood of figuring out where all the interim phases are between the starting point and the end state.

Exercise: The Smallest Testable Unit

I developed this exercise for planning failure drills (better known to some software engineers as chaos experiments). I eventually ended up repurposing it as an interview question to assess a candidate's ability to design a road map for a transition.

We start with a large goal we want to reach. For example, suppose we have a web application where secrets are kept in a plaintext configuration file. Three decades ago, that would have been the right way to build an application, but now it's not secure enough. Any number of solutions will improve security, but the organization may not be able to use all of them. This is a typical problem with legacy modernizations: the ideal solution is dependent on conditions that are either not present or not possible. Leaders have to decide whether to compromise on another solution or invest time and energy resolving the dependencies of the preferred solution.

You might be familiar with the expression *yak shaving*. It's when every problem has another problem that must be solved before it can be addressed. In a way, the smallest testable unit exercise is a yak-shaving exercise. You advance through each stage by asking the question "What do we need to do this, and how can we test that we have it?" For the previous example, the road map might look like this:

- We need to move secrets to a secure secret management solution. To do that, we need to know how many secrets we have, where they are in code, and who or what needs to use them.

- We can figure out who needs to use our current secrets by carefully logging access to them. To do that, we need a way to aggregate logs and search them. We should take care not to log actual secrets, just the request for them.

- We can test whether we have the ability to aggregate and search logs by having various parts of the application write distinctive messages to the logs and check where those messages end up. To do that, we need access to the application source code.

- We can test whether we have access to the source code by finding the repository, reading the code, and attempting to submit a change to it. To do that, we need some kind of version control solution.

And so on, and so forth.

Done well, the candidate plans the roadmap out backward, starting at the end state and identifying smaller and smaller units of change. With each step, we are designing tests to find weaknesses in the organization's operational excellence that we can resolve. It's important that our roadmap is structured around proving we have something with a simple test, rather than steps that assert we do. On large projects, it's easy for people to become confused or misreport the ground truth. It is useful to know how a leader would construct a test to verify information.

A leader with low tolerance for ambiguity either doesn't see these blockers or will not acknowledge them, so she sends a top-down directive mandating the new solution. Engineering whips up a hack or a workaround to handle the blockers or else just ignores the top-down directive, and efforts to improve the legacy system stall.

Structuring the Team to Account for Past Failure

Legacy modernizations are never about just one team or one leader. Legacy systems survive because they are important; processes tend to grow around important systems, and organizations tend to grow around those processes. Even if you chose to run one team specifically for the modernization itself, the work of that one team will rely on and influence other teams.

The three effective structures for modernization are as follows:

Teams that mirror existing components. If there's a short history of failure, you may be able to trust the current division of labor to carry the day. The teams consist of either all or parts of existing teams, so coordination between them takes the form of a cross-functional meeting group populated by either the leads of each existing component or someone appointed by the component to represent them. More than any other structure, this option relies heavily on interpersonal connections. If cliques and rivalries have begun to form in the organization, it will be hard to keep the group focused.

Lead team and subgroups. With this model, a lead team shapes the high-level view of the modernization effort and then dispatches tasks to the subgroups who are empowered to make any and all decisions on the details of how they implement those instructions. The more a particular modernization project has a track record of failure, the more I like to form a distinction between our effort and business as usual. That means this structure can take the shape of an architecture group advising business components (which we might already have set up), or we can pull people off their normal teams for a short period of time. It is better to avoid slotting the same people into the same roles, and you will likely see an immediate boost of motivation provided the shuffling of roles is made in good faith and the objectives are clear.

As I mentioned in Chapter 6, nothing says you're serious about accomplishing something more effectively than changing people's scenery.

Consult the "Solution: Code Yellow" on page 116 for more information on how this structure can work.

One embedded team. When the history of failure is long, sometimes the best option is to embed people within existing teams for the sole purpose of implementing solutions. In this model, one team decides on the plan and then dispatches its members to different components around the organization to work on the solution. The trick to getting this right is identity. The members of the embedded team must have strong bonds of camaraderie with each other. They must feel like one team. They should treat their host teams with compassion and empathy, but they also should consider the host teams more like clients or customers rather than as peers.

This is not the same as pulling representatives from every team into a joint committee. In the committee solution, the individual is bonded to her home team, while having no particular attachment to her colleagues on the committee. With an embedded team, the dynamic should be reversed.

Implementing these three structures is an exercise in itself to help figure out organically how the organization should self-organize around the new system once completed. Conway's law is ultimately about communication and incentives. The incentive side can be covered by giving people a pathway to prestige and career advancement that complements the modernization effort. The only way to design communication pathways is actually to give people something to communicate about. In each case, we allow the vision for the new organization to reveal itself by designing structures that encourage new communication pathways to form in response to our modernization challenges. As the work continues, those communication pathways begin to solidify, and we can begin documentation and formalizing new teams or roles. In this way, we sidestep the anxiety of reorganizing. The workers determine where they belong based on how they adapt to problems; workers typically left out are given time and space to learn new skills or prove themselves in different roles, and by the time the new organization structure is ratified by leadership, everyone already has been working that way for a couple months.

Choose your modernization team structure based on how much organizational change you think will be needed to make the new system maintainable.

Leaving teams as they are supposes that the abstractions of the new system will match those of the old system. There will not be new responsibilities; there will not be new roles. The only things that change from the old system to the new are implementation details like language or tool selection. Many migrations will look like this.

Having a lead team with subgroups assumes that there will be overarching problems that no one existing team is empowered to fix or has all the necessary information to fix. By the time the new system is completed, new teams may have developed around those issues. For example, the organization might realize that new services need to be developed or that to enforce good practices across the engineering organization, they need internal tooling. With this structure, we know some parts of our engineering group will remain the same, and some parts of it will change, but we don't know exactly how.

Finally, the embedded team sets the precedent of injecting expertise as needed into other teams. I use this structure when the goal state of the new system is significantly different from the old system. When there's that much change, technology and practices that are completely foreign to existing engineers usually are being introduced. Moving off mainframes, shutting down a data center in favor of the cloud, rolling out SRE, or incorporating orchestration are all examples of modernization challenges where there is likely to be a skills gap on the existing teams. The expert being injected to advise and assist will start the process of forming new teams by figuring out how the work the old team needs to do gets split up. For example, if the modernization effort involves a new piece of technology, not everyone on the team will need to reach the same proficiency level with it. Rather than a senior manager deciding who will go where, the organization lets the existing team work on it and sees who develops an aptitude.

What you don't want to do is draw a new organization chart based on your vision for how teams will be arranged with the new system. You don't want to do this for the same reason that you don't want to start product development with everything designed up front. Your concept of what the new system will look like will be wrong in some minor ways you can't possibly foresee. You don't want to lock in your team to a structure that will not fit their needs.

Instead, ask yourself who needs to collaborate with whom for various stages of the modernization project to work, and pick a structure that makes this communication easy.

Exercise: In-Group/Out-Group

Who needs to communicate with whom may not be clear when you get started. This is an exercise I use to help reveal where the communication pathways are or should be. I give everyone a piece of paper with a circle drawn on it. The instructions are to write down the names of the people whose work they are dependent on inside the circle (in other words, "If this person fell behind schedule, would you be blocked?") and the names of people who give them advice outside the circle. If there's no one specific person, they can write a group or team name or a specific role, like frontend engineer, instead.

Then I compare the results across each team. In theory, those inside the circle are people with whom the engineer needs to collaborate closely. Each result should resemble that engineer's actual team with perhaps a few additions or deletions based on current issues playing out. Outside the circle should be all the other teams. Experts not on the team should be seen as interchangeable with other experts in the same field.

Small variations will exist from person to person, but if the visualizations that people produce don't look like their current teams, you know your existing structure does not meet your communication needs.

You can modify this exercise to look at the communication needs of the new system instead of the existing one by focusing the research question on a future work stream. Instead of which people might be blockers or advisors generally, ask people to visualize the in-group and out-group in terms of a specific modernization task.

Takeaways

This chapter covers a lot of ground. Design thinking is a rich landscape with lots of insight and strategy of value to the task of legacy modernization. I have tried to demonstrate enough of that value to encourage you to bring a designer into your fold if you don't already have one. To review, here are the takeaways you should have from this chapter:

- Design is problem setting. Incorporating it into your process will help your teams become more resilient.

- By themselves, technical conversations tend to incentivize people to maintain status by criticizing ideas. Design can help mitigate those effects by giving conversations the structure of a game and a path to winning.

- Legacy modernizations are ultimately transitions and require leaders with high tolerance for ambiguity.

- Conway's law doesn't mean you should design your organization to look like the technology you want. It means you should pay attention to how the organization structure incentivizes people to behave. These forces will determine what the technology looks like.

- Don't design the organization; let the organization design itself by choosing a structure that facilitates the communication teams will need to get the job done.

In the next chapter, I'll continue to explore the concept of communication by tackling the issue of breaking changes and how to keep them from blocking progress forward.

BREAKING CHANGES

In government, we had a saying, "The only thing the government hates more than change is the way things are." The same inertia lingers over legacy systems. It is impossible to improve a large, complex, debt-ridden system without breaking it. If you're lucky, the resulting outages will be resolved quickly and result in minimum data loss, but they will happen.

Another expression that was popular among my colleagues in government was "air cover." To have air cover was to have confidence that the organization would help your team survive such inevitable breakages. It was to have someone who trusted and understood the value of change and could protect the team. As a team lead, my job was to secure that air cover. When I moved back to the private sector, I applied the same principles as a manager—networking, relationship building, recruiting, doing favors—so I could give my team members the safety and security necessary to do the hard jobs for which I had hired them.

In this chapter, I explore the concept of breaking changes. How do you sell dangerous changes while being honest about their risks? When should you break stuff, and how do you recover quickly?

But, I want to start with the concept of air cover. Business writers sometimes refer to "psychological safety," which is another great way to describe the same concept. To do effective work, people need to feel safe and supported. Leadership buy-in is one part of creating the feeling of air cover, but for air cover to be effective, it has to alter an organization's perception of risk.

Risk is not a static number on a spreadsheet. It's a feeling that can be manipulated, and while we may justify that feeling with statistics, probabilities, and facts, our perception of level of risk often bears no relationship to those data points.

Being Seen

A year or two ago, I was invited to give a guest lecture on working with software engineers at Harvard's Kennedy School for Government. When it came time to give practical advice, the first slide on my deck said in big letters, "How do people get seen?"

Being seen is not specifically about praise. It's more about being noticed or acknowledged, even if the sentiment expressed in that acknowledgment is neutral. Just as status-seeking behavior influences what people say in meetings, looking to be seen influences what risks people are willing to tolerate. Fear of change is all about perception of risk. People construct risk assessments based on two vectors: level of punishment or reward and odds of getting caught.

Of those two, people are more sensitive to changes in odds of getting caught than level of punishment or reward.[1] If you want to deter crime, increase the perception that the police are effective, and criminals will be caught. If you want to incentivize behavior, pay attention to what behaviors get noticed within an organization.

---

[1] Daniel S. Nagin, "Deterrence in the Twenty-First Century," *Crime and Justice* 42 (2013): 199–263, *https://doi.org/10.1086/670398*.

Organizations can pay a lot of lip service to good behaviors but still not notice them. Being seen is not about matching an organization's theoretical ideals, it's about what your peers will notice. It's easy for the organization's rhetoric to be disconnected from the values that govern the work environment. What colleagues pay attention to are the real values of an organization. No matter how passionate or consistent the messaging, attention from colleagues will win out over the speeches.

The specific form of acknowledgment also matters a lot. Positive reinforcement in the form of social recognition tends to be a more effective motivator than the traditional incentive structure of promotions, raises, and bonuses. Behavioral economist Dan Ariely attributes this to the difference between social markets and traditional monetary-based markets.[2] Social markets are governed by social norms (read: peer pressure and social capital), and they often inspire people to work harder and longer than much more expensive incentives that represent the traditional work-for-pay exchange. In other words, people will work hard for positive reinforcement; they might not work harder for an extra thousand dollars.

Ariely's research suggests that even evoking the traditional market by offering small financial incentives to work harder causes people to stop thinking about the bonds between them and their colleagues and makes them think about things in terms of a monetary exchange[3]—which is a colder, less personal, and often less emotionally rewarding space.

The idea that one needs a financial reward to want to do a good job for an organization is cynical. It assumes bad faith on the part of the employee, which builds resentment. Traditional incentives have little positive influence, therefore, because they disrupt what was otherwise

---

[2] James Heyman and Dan Ariely, "Effort for Payment: A Tale of Two Markets," *Psychological Science* 15, no. 11 (2004): 787–793, *https://doi.org/10.1111/j.0956-7976.2004.00757.x.*

[3] Dan Ariely, *Predictably Irrational: The Hidden Forces That Shape Our Decisions* (New York: HarperCollins, 2008).

a personal relationship based on trust and respect. Behavioralist Alfie Kohn puts it this way:

> Punishment and rewards are two sides of the same coin. Rewards have a punitive effect because they, like outright punishment, are manipulative. "Do this and you'll get that" is not really very different from "Do this or here's what will happen to you." In the case of incentives, the reward itself may be highly desired; but by making that bonus contingent on certain behaviors, managers manipulate their subordinates, and that experience of being controlled is likely to assume a punitive quality over time.[4]

Here's an example of this in practice. When I worked for USDS, my boss constantly complained about people doing the exact opposite of what he told them time and time again was what he wanted them to do. Specifically, he kept telling teams not to take systems away from the organizations that owned them. USDS operated, at least in theory, on a consulting model. We were supposed to assist and advise agencies, not adopt their legacy systems long term without any exit plan. My boss complained about this approach over and over again. He could not understand why people kept gravitating toward a strategy that was more difficult, less likely to succeed, and against his wishes.

Every week, we had a staff meeting where people demoed what they were working on and gave status updates. Inevitably, USDSers would censor their updates, wanting to talk about things only once they had achieved success. This meant product launches. All we talked about at staff meetings were product launches. Eventually, this convention became self-reinforcing. People began to think they shouldn't talk about a project before it had a launch coming up or a milestone reached, that the little wins were not worth mentioning.

---

4. Alfie Kohn, "Why Incentive Plans Cannot Work," *Harvard Business Review,* September/ October 1993, *https://hbr.org/1993/09/why-incentive-plans-cannot-work.*

The problem was that most USDS projects involved old systems where the solutions would take months of untangling, even if the government bureaucracy wasn't a factor. Talking only about product launches meant certain teams might work for a full year on something before their peers ever heard about their projects.

My boss's advice of not taking things away from the organizations that owned them was great advice for long-term sustainability, but it would mean feelings of isolation as colleagues talked about their work and you had nothing to contribute, because it would take months to get to a product launch. What's the best way to speed that up? Take over the system, remove or otherwise bypass the government client who owns it, and bring in a team of bright young USDSers to do all the work. This got products to launch quicker, but handing them off to the government stakeholders became close to impossible. They didn't know anything about the new system. This is what my boss was trying to prevent, but people ignored his advice to prioritize the methods that were going to get them seen by their peers early and often.

When we realized this, we decided to schedule a 10-minute block at the end of every staff meeting for "kudos." Kudos were acknowledgments and congratulations of small wins throughout the organization. Did a meeting go well? Write a kudos. Did someone go above and beyond the call of duty to fix something? Write a kudos. Did a team show integrity and resolve through a project failure? Write a kudos. We would collect all the kudos in a specific repository throughout the week, and then at the end of the staff meeting, someone would read them all out loud.

Given a choice between a monetary incentive and a social one, people will almost always choose the behavior that gets them the social boost. So when you're examining why certain failures are considered riskier than others, an important question to ask yourself is this: How do people get seen here? What behaviors and accomplishments give them an opportunity to talk about their ideas and their work with their colleagues and be acknowledged?

If you want to improve people's tolerance for certain types of risks, change where the organization lands on those two critical vectors of rewards and acknowledgment. You have four options: increase the odds that good behavior will get noticed (especially by peers), decrease the odds that bad outcomes will get noticed, increase the rewards for good behavior, or decrease the punishment for bad outcomes. All of these will alter an organization's perception of risk and make breaking changes easier.

Note the distinction between good *behavior* and bad *outcomes*. When deciding how they should execute on a given set of tasks, workers consider two questions: How does the organization want me to behave? And, will I get punished if things go wrong despite that correct behavior? If you want people to do the right thing despite the risk, you need to accept that failure.

One of the most famous examples of these principles in play to raise engineering standards is Etsy's 3-Arm Sweater award.[5] The image of the 3-Arm Sweater is used throughout Etsy to signify a screw-up. It is featured prominently on its 404 File Not Found page, for example. The 3-Arm Sweater award is given out to the engineer who triggers the worst outage. Celebrating failure wasn't just an annual tradition; Etsy employees had an email list to broadcast failure stories company-wide.[6] Because Etsy wanted to establish a *just culture*, where people learned from mistakes together instead of trying to hide them, the company found ways to integrate the acknowledgment of those behaviors into day-to-day operations. These practices helped Etsy scale its technology to 40 million unique visitors every month.[7]

---

[5] Howard Greenstein, "Build a Culture That Celebrates Mistakes," Inc., June 19, 2012, *https://www.inc.com/howard-greenstein/build-a-start-up-tech-culture-that-celebrates-mistakes.html.*

[6] Ibid.

[7] Knowledge@Wharton, "Here's How Etsy Plans to Scale Without Losing Its Crafty, Handmade Aesthetic," Business Insider, May 10, 2012, *https://www.businessinsider.com/heres-how-etsy-plans-to-scale-without-losing-its-crafty-handmade-aesthetic-2012-5.*

If you want your team to be able to handle breaking things, pay attention to what the organization celebrates. Blameless postmortems and just culture are a good place to start, because they both manipulate how people perceive failure and establish good engineering practices.

Who Draws the Line?

But, can blameless postmortems ever *really* be blameless?

In 2008, system safety researcher Sidney Dekker published an article titled "Just Culture: Who Gets to Draw the Line?"[8] Dekker's article addresses whether true "blameless" postmortems, where no one was ever punished for errors, are the desired end state of just cultures. People want psychological safety, but they also want accountability. No one wants to excuse actual negligence, but if there's a line between mistakes that should be blameless and those where people should be held accountable, who should be able to draw it?

A popular exercise with first-year computer science students is to write a hypothetical program instructing a robot to walk across the room. Students soon find that the simplest of instructions, when taken literally, can lead to unexpected results, and the purpose of the exercise is to teach them something about algorithms as well as what assumptions computers can and cannot make.

Safety researchers like Dekker view organizational procedures largely the same way. Prescribed safety, security, and reliability processes are useful only if operators can exercise discretion when applying them. When organizations take the ability to adapt away from the software engineers in charge of a system, any gap in what procedure covers becomes an Achilles heel.

---

8. Sidney W. A. Dekker, "Just Culture: Who Gets to Draw the Line?" *Cognition, Technology & Work* 11 (2008): 177–185, *https://doi.org/10.1007/s10111-008-0110-7*.

That's why the issue of who gets to draw the line is so critical to a just culture. The closer the line-drawing pattern is to the people who must maintain the system, the greater the resilience. The further away, the more bureaucratic and dysfunctional.

Also, the line is never drawn once; it is actively renegotiated. No rule maker can possibly predict every conceivable situation or circumstance an organization and its technology might confront. So the line between blameless behavior and behavior that people should be held accountable for is redrawn. These corrections can be influenced by cultural, social, or political forces.

Just as understanding how people get seen is important to constructing incentives that moderate people's perception of risk, understanding who gets to draw the line between mistakes that are acceptable and those that are not is important to understanding how privilege is distributed around an organization. The highest probability of success comes from having as many people engaged and empowered to execute as possible. Those who cannot draw the line or renegotiate the placement of the line are the organization members with the least privilege and the most in need of investment to get the full benefit of their efforts.

Building Trust Through Failure

The suggestion that failure should be embraced or that a modernization team should deliberately break something makes people uncomfortable. The assumption is that failure is a loss—failure always leaves you worse off.

Or does it?

The science paints a much more complex picture. Although a system that constantly breaks, or that breaks in unexpected ways without warning, will lose its users' trust, the reverse isn't necessarily true. A system that never breaks doesn't necessarily inspire high degrees of trust.

Italian researchers Cristiano Castelfranchi and Rino Falcone have been advancing a general model of trust in which trust degrades over time, regardless of whether any action has been taken to violate that trust.[9] People take systems that are too reliable for granted. Under Castelfranchi and Falcone's model, maintaining trust doesn't mean establishing a perfect record; it means continuing to rack up observations of resilience. If a piece of technology is so reliable it has been completely forgotten, it is not creating those regular observations. Through no fault of the technology, the user's trust in it will slowly deteriorate.

Those of us who work in the field of legacy modernization see this happen all the time. Organizations become gung-ho to remove a system that has been stable and efficient for decades because it is old, and therefore, management has become convinced that a meltdown is imminent.

We also see this happen on more modern systems. Google has repeatedly promoted the notion that when services are overperforming their SLOs, teams are encouraged to create outages to bring the performance level down.[10] The rationale for this is that perfectly running systems create a false sense of security that lead other engineering teams to stop building proper fail-safes. This might be true, but a different way to look at it is that the more a service overperforms, the less confident Google's SREs become in overall system stability.

The idea that something is more likely to go wrong only because there's been a long gap when nothing has gone wrong is a version of the *gambler's fallacy*. It's not the lack of failure that makes a system more likely to fail, it's the inattention in the maintenance schedule or the failure to test appropriately or other cut corners. Whether the assumption that a too reliable system is in danger is sensible depends on what evidence people are calling on to determine the odds of failure.

[9.] Cristiano Castelfranchi and Rino Falcone, *Trust Theory* (Hoboken, NJ: Wiley, 2009).

[10.] Chris Jones, John Wilkes, and Cody Smith, "Service Level Objectives," in *Site Reliability Engineering: How Google Runs Production Systems*, ed. Betsy Beyer, Chris Jones, Jennifer Petoff, and Niall Richard Murphy (Sebastopol, CA: O'Reilly Media, 2016). See also "Site Reliability Engineering," Google, accessed January 8, 2020, *https://landing.google.com/sre/*.

The gambler's fallacy is one of those logical fallacies that is so pervasive, it shows up in all kinds of weird ways. In 1796, for example, a French philosopher documented how expecting fathers felt anxiety and despair when other local women gave birth to sons because they were convinced it lowered their likelihood of having a son within the same period.[11]

For this reason, the occasional outage and problem with a system—particularly if it is resolved quickly and cleanly—can actually boost the user's trust and confidence. The technical term for this effect is the *service recovery paradox*.[12]

Researchers haven't been able to pin down the exact nature of the service recovery paradox—why it happens in some cases but not others—therefore, you shouldn't take things as far as trying to optimize customer satisfaction by *triggering* outages. That being said, what we do know is that recovering fast and being transparent about the nature of the outage and the resolution often improves relationships with stakeholders. Factoring in the boost to psychological safety and productivity that just culture creates, technical organizations shouldn't shy away from breaking things on purpose. Under the right conditions, the cost of user trust is minimal, and the benefits might be substantial.

Breaking Change vs. Breaking

Before I go into the nitty-gritty details of deliberately breaking systems, I should acknowledge that I'm using the phrase *breaking change* to refer to *all changes* that break a system. Breaking change is not normally that broad.

---

[11] Greg Barron and Stephen Leider, "The Role of Experience in the Gambler's Fallacy," *Journal of Behavioral Decision Making* 23, no. 1 (2009): 117–129, *https://doi.org/10.1002/bdm.676*.

[12] Anupam Krishna, G. S. Dangayach, and Sonal Sharma, "Service Recovery Paradox: The Success Parameters," *Global Business Review* 15, no. 2 (June 2014): 263–277, *https://doi.org/10.1177/0972150914523567*.

Typically, what we mean when we say breaking change is a violation of the data contract that impacts external users. A breaking change is something that requires customers or users to upgrade or modify their own systems to keep everything working. It is a change that breaks technology owned by other organizations.

For the sake of convenience, I'm using the expression *breaking change* here to refer to any kind of change—internally or externally—that alters system functionality in a negative way. The rest of this chapter discusses both the changes we make as part of deprecations and redesigns that break contacts on external-facing APIs and the changes we make when seeking to reduce a system's overall complexity.

Why Break Things on Purpose?

It's unlikely that any significant legacy modernization project can complete without breaking the system at least once. But, breaking a system as an unfortunate consequence of other changes, knowing there's a risk that a break might occur, and deliberately breaking things on purpose are different scenarios. I'm arguing that your organization shouldn't just embrace resilience over risk aversion, but it should also occasionally break things on purpose.

What kind of scenarios justify breaking things on purpose? The most common one when dealing with legacy systems is loss of institutional memory. On any old system, one or two components exist that no one seems to know exactly what they do. If you are seeking to minimize the system's complexity and restore context, such knowledge gaps can't just be ignored. Mind you, the situations when you can't figure out what a component is doing from studying logs or digging up old documentation tend to be rare, but they do happen. Provided the system doesn't control nuclear weapons, turning the component off and seeing what breaks is a tool that should be available when all other avenues are exhausted.

Having a part of a system that no one understands is a weakness, so avoiding the issue for fear of breaking things should not be considered the safer choice. Using failure as a tool to make systems and the organizations that run them stronger is one of the foundational concepts behind resilience engineering. It's important to know how each part of a system works in a variety of conditions, including how interactions between parts work. Unfortunately, no one person can hold all of that information in his or her head. Knowledge about a system must be regularly shared among the different operational units of a technical organization. An organization needs processes to expose relevant details and scenarios, communicate them, and judge their significance. That's why the second reason to break things on purpose is to verify that what an organization believes about its system is actually true. Resilience engineering tests—also called *failure drills*—look to trigger failure strategically so that the true behavior of the system can be documented and verified.

The simplest and least threatening of failure drills is to restore from backup. Remember, if an organization has never restored from backup, it does not have working backups. Waiting for an actual outage to figure that out is not a safer strategy than running a failure drill at a time you've chosen, supervised by your most experienced engineers.

You can justify any failure test the same way. Is it better to wait for something to fail and hope you have the right resources and expertise at the ready? Or is it better to trigger failure at a time when you can plan resources, expertise, and impact in advance? You don't know that something doesn't work the way you intended it to until you try it.

Projecting Impact

Two types of impact are relevant to failure tests. The first is technical impact: the likelihood of cascading failures, data corruption, or dramatic changes in security or stability. The second is user impact: How many people are negatively affected and to what degree?

Technical impact will be the harder of the two to project. You should have some idea of how different parts of the system are coupled and where the complexity is in your system from exercises in previous chapters; now you'll want to put that information into a model of potential failures.

A good way to start is with a 4+1 architectural view model. Developed by Philippe Kruchten,[13] a 4+1 architectural view model breaks an architectural model into separate diagrams that reflect the concerns of one specific viewpoint.

- *Logical view* maps out how end users experience a system. This might take the form of a state diagram, where system state changes (such as updates to the database) are tracked along user behavior. When the user clicks a particular button, what happens? What actions could the user take from that point, and how would the system state adjust?

- *Process view* looks at what the system is doing and in what order. Process views are similar to logical views except the orientation is flipped. Instead of focusing on what the user is doing, the focus is on what processes the machine is initiating and why.

- *Development view* is the system how software engineers see it. The architecture is broken out by components reflecting the application code structure.

- *Physical view* shows us our systems as represented across physical hardware. What actually gets sent across the network? What else lives on the same servers?

The +1 in the 4+1 architecture refers to scenarios. *Scenarios* take a small sample of features that can be connected to a specific technique or functionality and focus on it. In other words, these are use cases.

[13.] Philippe Kruchten, "Architectural Blueprints—The '4+1' View Model of Software Architecture," *IEEE Software* 12 no. 6 (November 1995): 42–50.

These views are easier to understand by example. Let's consider a hypothetical system where users upload scanned documents that are converted to text files. These text files are tagged automatically based on their context, but users may edit both this metadata and the transcription itself.

The logical view of this system might look like Figure 8-1.

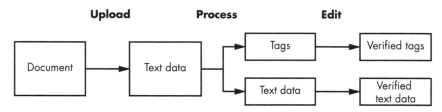

Figure 8-1: *Logical view, a state machine*

We model the state of the data as it goes from document to processed verified output. Each of the stages is kicked off by a user action, and it's easy to see the functional requirements of the system.

The process view, on the other hand, might look something like Figure 8-2.

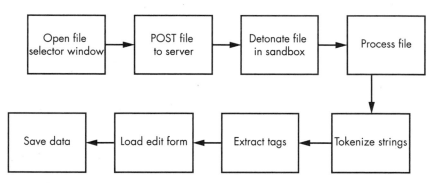

Figure 8-2: *Process view, the technical processes being performed*

Processing a file begins with triggering the interface to select the file for the user's computer. Upon receiving the file, the server downloads it into a sandbox to ensure it's safe. While processing, text data is tokenized so that tags of the most common significant words can be extracted. Then we load that data into an edit form so the user can validate it.

Although the two views describe the same system with the same set of functions, they highlight different things. The process view contains requirements around ensuring the file being uploaded is safe and how the tags are identified that are not visible to the user, but without the logical view, we might not realize that the intention of the system is that the data should not be considered final until the user has verified it.

Kruchten developed the 4+1 architectural view model because he observed that traditional architectural diagrams tried to capture all the perspectives in one visualization. As a result, instead of enriching and deepening our ability to reason about a system, knowledge gaps were created where one view was emphasized over all others.

For example, the impacts of a broken sandbox are obvious on the process view, but they do not even register on the logical view. Whereas the logical view highlights tags and text as separate things that might break independently of one another, the process view does not reveal this.

The development and physical views have a similar relationship. Figure 8-3 shows what this hypothetical system might look like in a development view.

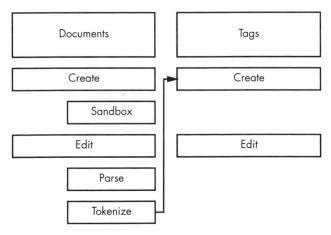

Figure 8-3: *Development view, how the code is structured*

Code is organized into two classes: Documents and Tags. Each class has a set of methods reflecting a Create, Read, Update, and Delete (CRUD) structure. This system saves the document as soon as we've verified that it's safe, so that if the parser fails, we don't lose data. It tokenizes as it parses and creates tags after.

The physical view might look more like Figure 8-4.

Users access the system from browsers on their computers. The web application runs on a server that interacts with a separate VM for sandboxing, an object store for preprocessed documents, and a database for post-processed data.

Each of these views is different, and by considering them together, we get a clearer picture of the different ways that one component of the system might fail and what that failure would affect.

Once we've modeled the system and feel confident that we understand it, we can flesh out our analysis of potential failures by collecting data from the running system to try to determine how many stakeholders would be affected in case of failure and the likelihood of failure happening at all.

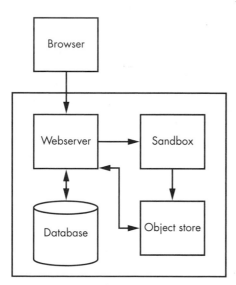

Figure 8-4: Physical view, servers in a cloud environment

The simplest and most obvious place to start is with the system's logs. Is a log produced when this component of the system is active, and do we know what triggered it, when it was triggered, how long it ran, or other metadata? If we don't have logs, can we add them? A week or two of data will not give you a complete picture, but it will validate what an outage would impact and clarify the order of magnitude.

Another trick to estimating impact is to consider whether the mitigation can actually be automated. We had this issue around templates once. For security reasons, we wanted to standardize on one templating language. We needed our users to convert their custom templates and didn't want to spend months communicating and negotiating with customers, so we built a tool that did the conversion for the customer and tested that the new templates rendered identically.

Finally, there's the most extreme method I mentioned before: turn the component off and see who complains. What if the request leaves your network and you can't tell what the receiver is doing with it, if anything? In those cases, you need to chip away at the challenge until you've defined the impact. A micro-outage is similar to "turn it off and see who complains," except that you remove the asset only for a small period of time and do not wait for a complaint to turn it back on.

The Kill Switch

As a result of your analysis, you should have a general idea of what is likely to go wrong. Given that information, part of the plan before deliberately breaking a component of a system should be establishing termination criteria. That is to say, if the breakage triggers impacts beyond a certain level, when and how do you revert the breakage? Having a rollback strategy is important for any kind of change to an operational system, but it's effective only if everyone understands what the tolerance for failure really is.

Setting the criteria and process for undoing the break before anything is damaged gives people the ability to take on the risk with confidence.

Communicating Failure

Of course, it's not very diplomatic to break something that will affect colleagues and users without letting them know. Some level of communication is usually needed, but how much and with whom depends on the objectives of the breaking change.

If you are breaking something to test the system's resilience, providing too much information can limit the effectiveness of the drill. The whole point of a failure drill is to test whether procedures for recovery work as expected. Real failures rarely announce themselves or provide a detailed description of how they are triggered.

Before a failure drill, it is not necessary to notify external users at all. In theory, your organization will recover successfully, and users will experience no negative impacts. Internal stakeholders, including system users and other engineering teams, should be notified that there will be a failure drill on a specific part of the system, but they don't need to know how long the outage will last, when exactly it will be, or the nature of the failure to be triggered. If the drill is a routine test of backups and fail-safes, a week's notice is usually acceptable. If the drill will affect areas of the system with unclear or complex recovery paths or if the drill is testing human factors in the recovery process, more notice is a good idea. You want to give teams enough time to assess the potential impact on the parts of the system they own and double-check their mitigation strategies. Typically, I recommend no more than 90 days' advance notice for the most elaborate failure drills. If you provide too much time, people will procrastinate to the point where it is as if they were given no advanced notice at all. If you give too little notice, teams will need to stop normal development work to be ready in time.

It's different if you are breaking something with the intention of decommissioning it or otherwise leaving it permanently altered. In that case, it is more important to communicate the change to external users. The traditional way to do this is to set a date for decommissioning the specific feature or service, declare it deprecated, and notify users a few months in advance. How much time to give users depends on how complex the migration away from the deprecated feature is likely to be. I don't think there's much value in providing years of notice versus months for the same reason I don't usually give internal teams more than 90 days of notice for a failure drill: more time often leads to more procrastination.

If you are particularly unlucky, you might find yourself in a situation where you cannot inform users with an email, a phone call, or even a letter. You may not even know exactly who the users are. In those situations, you either have to get a little creative or take your chances that a component that looks unused actually is.

Posting a deprecation notice somewhere that users are likely to look for information is one solution. One time, when we could find no other way to figure out who was using a specific API, we put a message in the API itself. Since the attribute we wanted to get rid of happened to be a string, we just changed the content of the string to a message saying that, for security reasons, we would no longer be providing that value and to contact customer support for more information.

But, whatever the method, the most important part of your communication strategy is that you carry out the breaking change when you said you were going to do it. If you hesitate or delay, users will simply not bother migrating at all, and the impact of the breakage will be much more damaging.

Once you set a date for failure, whether it's a drill or a permanent decommissioning, you need to honor that commitment.

Failure Is a Best Practice

To summarize, people's perception of risk is not static, and it's often not connected to the probability of failure so much as it is the potential feeling of rejection and condemnation from their peers. Since social pressures and rewards are better incentives than money and promotions, you can improve your odds of success by learning how to manipulate an organization's perception of risk.

The first task is to understand what behaviors get individuals within an organization acknowledged. Those are the activities that people will ultimately prioritize. If they are not the activities that you think will advance your modernization process, explore constructs, traditions, and—there's no better word for it—rituals that acknowledge complementary activities.

The second task is to look at which part of the organization gets to determine when the operator can exercise discretion and deviate from defined procedure. Those are the people who set the ratio of blamelessness to accountability in handling failure. Those are the people who will grant air cover and who need to buy in to any breaking change strategy for it to be successful. Once that air cover is established, anxiety around failure tends to relax.

Once you know how to manipulate the organization's perception of risk, successfully managing the break is all about preparation. While you will not be able to predict everything that could go wrong, you should be able to do enough research to give your team the ability to adapt to the unknown with confidence. At a minimum, everyone should know and understand the criteria for rolling back a breaking change.

Failure does not necessarily jeopardize user trust. If the situation is quickly resolved and users receive clear and honest communication about the problem, the occasional failure can trigger the service recovery paradox and inspire greater user confidence.

Organizations should not shy away from failure, because failure can never be prevented. It can only be put off for a while or redirected to another part of the system. Eventually, every organization will experience failure. Embracing failure as a source of learning means that your team gains more experience and ultimately improves their skills mitigating negative impacts on users. Practicing recovering from failure, therefore, makes the team more valuable.

HOW TO FINISH

When I was working for the United Nations (UN), my boss at the time would regularly start conversations with the words "When the website is done . . ." to which I would respond, "The website is never done." I count among my accomplishments the fact that by the time I left the UN, people had bought in to the agile, iterative process that treats software as a living thing that needs to be constantly maintained and improved. They stopped saying "When the website is done . . ."

Technology is never done, but modernization projects can be. This chapter covers how to define success in a way that makes it clear when the modernization effort is completed and what to do next. In the beginning of a project, what success looks like can seem obvious, but often some people in an organization make assumptions about what success means that are different from the assumptions of others. Getting everyone on the same page and keeping everyone on the same page is critical to ensuring that the project crosses the finish line.

Revealing Assumptions

A fair number of broken systems end up that way because the units of the organization involved in the implementation saw their roles and how they contributed to the larger picture differently from one another. Any kind of modernization, rearchitecting, or rethinking of an existing technical system is a long game. Work will stretch on for months or years. For that reason, it is essential when you work on these projects that everyone on the team is able to answer this question: How do we know if it's getting better?

The team should know the long-term answer to that, but they should also know what better looks like within days or weeks from where they are now. This kind of work is a slog. To do it well, you have to maintain your own resilience. You have to be mindful of how people behave when they think a project is going poorly. The only thing harder than managing your own doubts is dealing with sabotage from colleagues who don't understand how much progress is being made because their expectations of what improvement will look like is different from other members of the team.

Approach 1: Success Criteria

Success doesn't happen quickly or all at once, which begs the question: How do you know whether a project is moving in the right direction? When I set success criteria with my teams (and usually my boss or other significant stakeholders), we first determine the time frame for evaluation. If two people agree that shipping a feature is an indication of success, they can still come into conflict if they disagree on the timeline. Shipping something in three months is not the same thing as shipping it in a week. For the person who believes the feature should be shipped in a week, a deploy much later feels like a warning sign. For the person who believes it should be shipped in a year, the same deploy is validation.

If you are familiar with *objectives and key results (OKRs)*, success criteria can take on a similar shape. First, you define your goal, and then, you define how you'll know that you've reached your goal. Except, OKRs usually focus on signs that the goal is completed, and success criteria should focus on signs that you're heading in the right direction.

The value of this strategy is that the criteria chosen indicates the approach that will be taken without anyone arguing about the approach. If the success criteria are all about implementing new features, it's unlikely the team is going to prioritize resolving any technical debt. If the success criteria are instead about decreasing the number of errors or speeding up minimum time to recover, the team has to focus on improving existing code. Whenever you can avoid having people argue about principles, philosophies, and other generalities of good engineering versus bad engineering, take advantage of it.

The same goal can have wildly different success criteria depending on the team's model. For example, a consulting model would focus on the client's ability to absorb and adopt process and best practices, not deploys. Consultants don't have much control over deploys, and the only way they get control is by not being consultants anymore. As software engineers, it is easy to fall into the trap of thinking that effective work will always look like writing code, but sometimes you get much closer to your desired outcome by teaching others to do the job rather than doing it yourself.

Example: Adding Continuous Integration/Continuous Deploy

Goal: Move service on to its own deploy pipeline.

Timeline: One quarter.

Success Criteria:

- Time to deploy drops by 20 percent.

- Any single person on the Service team can initiate and manage a deploy.

- Number of deploys in a week goes up.

Approach 2: Diagnosis-Policy-Actions

Developed by Richard Rumelt, this approach draws on the same information as success criteria but frames it a bit differently.[1] Information is represented in three segments: diagnosis, policy, and actions. *Diagnosis* is a definition of a problem being fixed. *Policy* refers to the boundaries of potential solutions—the rules about what the solution should involve doing or shouldn't involve doing. Finally, *actions* are the steps the team will take to solve the problem without violating their policy.

What's useful about Rumelt's approach is that it is more focused on what you're going to do and how you're going to do it. This might be better in situations when there is little consensus around what success should look like and no single authority to make that decision, but you may find this approach more difficult if your team struggles with road maps. The challenges of legacy modernization can be varied, intertwined, and politically complex. Teams might not agree on what success looks like, and they might also disagree on which tasks need to be executed to untangle problems. Rumelt's approach is better for situations when it is easier to reach agreement on the steps forward and their order, but harder to reach consensus on what signs of improvement will look like.

Example: Upgrading a Database

Diagnosis: Our database software is several versions out of date. The vendor won't provide support anymore.

Policy: We want to use blue-green deploys. We will never just turn one database version off and the other on all at once.

---

[1] Richard P. Rumelt, *Good Strategy Bad Strategy: The Difference and Why It Matters* (New York: Crown Business, 2011).

Actions:

- We will back up our data before each upgrade.
- We will upgrade to 3.2 on this date.
- We will update to 3.3 on this date.

Comparison

In terms of defining success, success criteria and diagnosis-policy-actions have different strengths and weaknesses. Success criteria connects modernization activities more directly to the value add they can demonstrate. It affords more flexibility in exactly what the team does by not prescribing a specific approach or set of tasks. It is an excellent exercise to run with bosses and any other oversight forces that might be inclined to micromanage a team. How to do something should be the decision of the people actually entrusted to do it. For that reason, the diagnosis-policy-actions approach is too detail oriented to help a team manage up. If the set of actions needs to be changed later, the team might be reluctant to do it and seem inconsistent in front of senior leadership. Discretion is so critical to success; don't forfeit your team's right to it by presenting implementation details for feedback if that's not requested. What leadership needs to know is what outcomes you're pushing for.

On the other hand, sometimes you know what better looks like but have no idea which set of actions will get you there. Research and experimentation might fail to signal a clear winner among competing road maps. One side of an organization might say this one thing needs to be fixed first, while another side might argue a completely different fix takes priority. If the situation can be resolved only by executive decision, the diagnosis-policy-action approach is a better fit. The same flexibility that makes success criteria effective at adapting to new information and changing tactics will create confusion when the team is undecided about the day-to-day work.

Marking Time

Defining what success looks like helps keep people on the same page, but since the success criteria and diagnosis-policy-actions approaches cut challenges into smaller accomplishments, you also need to stop people from losing faith in the significance of those small accomplishments. If the team feels like what they've succeeded in doing was not worth the time they invested in it, the effectiveness of your definition of success will be diminished.

What's to your advantage here is that the perception of time is just as variable as perception of risk. Finding a way to mark time is about finding a way to pull people out of day-to-day frustrations that slow down time and help them focus on the larger picture. My favorite way of marking time is bullet journaling. I have a book where every day I write down five things I am going to work on and how long I think they will take. Throughout the day, I check off those tasks as I complete them and jot down little notes with significant details. During slow periods, I often doodle in the margins or decorate pages with stickers I've gotten from vendors.

Whenever I flip two or three weeks back in my bullet journal, I am shocked by how much has changed. I've gotten so much more done than I realized. The tasks I've completed feel like months' worth of work. Sometimes I am shocked when looking only one week back in time.

Just as humans are terrible judges of probability, we're also terrible judges of time. What feels like ages might only be a few days. By marking time, we can realign our emotional perception of how things are going. Find some way to record what you worked on and when so the team can easily go back and get a full picture of how far they've come.

You might be tempted to say, "Oh, well, they can do that with our project management system." Except, project management tools are geared toward presenting one stream of work at a time. Marking time is more effective because of the more complete a picture it paints of one specific point in people's lives. Knowing that such-and-such ticket was closed on a certain day doesn't necessarily take me back to that moment. Sometimes a date is just a date. When you mark time, do so in a way that evokes memory, that highlights the feeling of distance between that moment and where the team is now.

Bullet journaling is effective for me because each page is a snapshot of everything that is on my mind at the time. I record work projects, personal projects, events and social activities, holidays, and illnesses. Anything that I expect to take up a large part of the day, I write down. Looking back on a project's progress with that information gives it a sense of context that I hadn't considered before. Once I consider it, I realize that I have not been standing in one place mindlessly banging my head against a wall. Bit by bit, piece by piece, I have made things better.

Postmortems on Success

For software engineers, a *postmortem* is a review done after an outage that explores the timeline of the failure, contributing factors, and the ultimate resolution in detail. We typically tack on the prefix "blameless" when referring to postmortems to emphasize that the purpose of doing a postmortem is to understand what went wrong, not to assign blame to a particular group or individual who made a mistake.

But postmortems are not specific to failure. If your modernization plan includes modeling your approach after another successful project, consider doing a postmortem on that project's success instead. Remember that we tend to think of failure as bad luck and success as skill. We do postmortems on failure because we're likely to see them as complex scenarios with a variety of contributing factors. We assume that success happens for simple, straightforward reasons.

In reality, success is no more or less complex than failure. You should use the same methodology to learn from success that you use to learn from failure.

Postmortem vs. Retrospective

Right now you might be thinking to yourself that your organization does do postmortems on success, you just call them *retrospectives*.

And, that's true. The post-sprint or post-launch retrospective does ask many of the same questions as a postmortem. However, I have yet to work with a technical organization that treated retrospectives and postmortems the same. In practice, retrospectives are much more informal. They do not generate reports for others to read—at least, not that I've ever seen. I do not know of any organizations that post their retrospectives online for the public to read. I've been in a lot of retrospectives where we've captured great information and had deep soul-searching conversations, but rarely have I seen that output leave the whiteboard and be shared with other teams.

As an industry, we *reflect* on success but *study* failure. Sometimes obsessively. I'm suggesting that if you're modeling your project after another team or another organization's success, you should devote some time to actually researching how that success came to be in the first place.

Running Postmortems

Before discussing writing postmortems on success, it might be useful to give an overview of how postmortems are run in technical organizations in general. The conventional postmortem format has a couple characteristics that are impractical outside incident response. For example, an outage happens quickly and ideally is resolved within hours, so creating a detailed timeline of events for that is an easier task than it would be for a project that has run for months.

A traditional postmortem describes the impact of the outage. The team discusses and documents what went well, what went poorly, and where people felt they got lucky. As mentioned, the postmortem often includes a detailed timeline of events around the incident response. These timelines break down what happened, when it happened, and who did what. Postmortems also do not usually reference people by name to protect them from blame. Instead, monikers like "SRE 1" or "Software Engineer 2" are used to identify individuals and the actions they took. The postmortem concludes with actionable steps for improvement. How can the organization improve the things that went poorly or build on the things that went well?

Postmortems are written by reviewing communications and interviewing team members. Then a final review meeting is held to present and verify the gathered information with the full team.

When running a postmortem on success, you have to weigh the investment of time and energy it will take to get that level of detail when the timeline stretches out over months instead of hours. Such efforts can become cumbersome and bureaucratic fast. Traditional postmortems are written by the software engineers who responded to the incident. These are people you want working on software, not writing reports.

For that reason, postmortems on success should be run like their lighter-weight cousin the retrospective, but documented with the philosophy of traditional postmortems. The value of the postmortem is not its level of detail, but the role it plays in knowledge sharing. Postmortems are about helping people not involved in the incident avoid the same mistakes. The best postmortems are also distributed outside the organization to cultivate trust through transparency.

Postmortems establish a record about what really happened and how specific actions affected the outcome. They do not document failure; they provide context. Postmortems on success should serve a similar purpose. Why was a specific approach or technique successful? Did the final strategy look like what the team had planned at the start? Your timeline in a postmortem for success should be built around these questions: How did the organization execute on the original strategy, how did the strategy change, when did those changes happen, and what triggered them?

Even the biggest successes have challenges that could have gone better and places where good fortune saved the day. Documenting those helps people evaluate the suitability of your approach for their own problems and ultimately reproduce your success.

If you're convinced the strategy from another organization will work for your issue, don't wait for those engineers to start doing postmortems. You can gather most of the information you need by taking people out for coffee. If there's an organization whose success you want to copy, spend a couple weeks interviewing people about their strategy using the postmortem's key questions.

What went well?

What could have gone better?

Where did you get lucky?

The Tale of Two War Rooms

I examine the contributing factors to success before finalizing a strategy, because I've seen organizations learn the wrong lessons from success. For example, an organization I was working with had a project that was hopelessly behind schedule. Not only did team members not have a realistic end date for even the smallest part of the project, they did not know why the project kept getting delayed in the first place. It was a large project that required a couple different organizational units to work together and share information. My consulting team was just rolling off a successful project that had faced a similar challenge. The organization had heard that on our project, we had arranged for representatives from each organizational unit to work out of the same room. For several months, instead of reporting to their offices or cubicles every day, this group sat down together in a large conference room with their laptops. This was a war room, not a meeting. Over time, the conference room looked more like an open plan co-working space.

The organization with the failing project decided to copy our strategy without talking to us or learning much about how this war room worked. A large conference room was booked for a month, and representatives from each affected operational unit were pulled in and told they had to work in that conference room together.

The organization didn't see the same results that we had, and eventually leadership representatives reached out and asked us why. Having neglected to research our success, they were forced to research their own failure again.

I understood their frustrations. After all, they had followed our process to the letter and gotten different results. Or at least, that's what the situation looked like from their perspective, but when they asked for my thoughts, I noticed they had missed one critical component of that war room.

They put the wrong people in it.

Working Groups vs. Committees

Throughout this book, I have suggested structures that involve one small group of people advising, planning for, and, at times, delegating work to a larger team. These are working groups. It has become popular as of late to use the term *working group* instead of the word *committee* because committee just sounds bureaucratic to most people. Committees have a reputation for not getting anything done or, worse, for building through compromise. A camel, the old expression goes, is a horse built by committee.

Working groups do not have this baggage, so people will often say they want to start a working group and turn around and start a committee instead—as if simply changing the name of a structure somehow makes the structure a more effective tool. Worse still, most people can no longer tell the difference between a working group and a committee. That was what the leaders had missed when they copied our successful strategy. The people in the war room of our project were a working group. The people in the war room of the failed project were a committee.

What exactly is the difference?

Working groups relax hierarchy to allow people to solve problems across organizational units, whereas committees both reflect and reinforce those organizational boundaries and hierarchies. Our war room was made up of software engineers and network administrators. We brought people who had to work together to implement the project into the same room to work next to one another instead of communicating over email, through bosses, and scheduling any number of conference calls.

The failed war room, on the other hand, was made up of executives. Rather than bringing together people who are peers but report up to different chains of command, this war room just mimicked the existing structure and the existing politics of the organization. Worse, the day to day of most of these executives consisted almost entirely of meetings. Instead of working shoulder to shoulder with colleagues, they used the war room as a place to throw their belongings as they ran in and out of other conference rooms to conduct business as usual.

Working groups are internally facing; the customers for a working group are the members of the working group itself. People join working groups to share their knowledge and experience with peers. They are effective because they establish a space for cross-organizational collaboration and troubleshooting. People on the implementation layer of an organization can bring their challenges to peers who have already experienced those challenges and hear their stories or bounce ideas off them. Sometimes this results in recommendations for leadership, but the primary purpose of a working group is to troubleshoot and evangelize across an organization or industry. Working groups are typically initiated and staffed by people on the implementation layer of the organization.

A committee is formed to advise an audience external to the committee itself, typically someone in senior leadership. Whereas the working group is open to those who consider themselves operating in the same space as the working group's topic area, committees are selected by the entity they will be advising and typically closed off to everyone else. That external authority decides the committee's scope and goals. The committee reports up to that external authority and exists solely for its benefit.

Committees also tend to have a lot of procedure around them, but the absence of chairpeople and *Robert's Rules of Order* does not make a committee a working group.

The model can have a fair amount of variation. A Code Yellow team, for example, might not be self-selecting, and ignoring its advice might have serious consequences, but the point of a Code Yellow team is to reorganize and redistribute resources temporarily across an organization. That team ultimately reports up to a leader who is closer to a peer than an executive. The important takeaway is working groups relax organizational boundaries while committees reinforce them.

There is little value in having senior managers represent their units in a war room. Since they are not implementing the technology themselves, they cannot speak to what compromises would unblock the project without going back to their own engineers. Our war room was successful because it shortened the distance those conversations had to travel. The failed war room added a game of telephone on top of the existing barriers to communication. One could never be sure that the message coming out of that war room was accurate or if the manager representing you had misunderstood an implementation detail.

Funny story: I would, from time to time, run war rooms filled with senior executives. It was a tactic I resorted to when the organization was in such a state of panic that senior leadership members were micromanaging their teams. Software engineers can't fix problems if they spend all their time in meetings giving their managers updates about the problems. The boot has to be moved off their necks.

In that situation, my team would typically run two war rooms: one where the engineers were solving problems together and one outfitted with lots of fancy dashboards where I was babysitting the senior executives. The most valuable skill a leader can have is knowing when to get out of the way.

Success Is Not Obvious If Undefined

Modernization projects without a clear definition of what success looks like will find themselves with a finish line that only moves further back the closer they get to it. Don't assume that success is obvious. Different members of your team may have different and competing visions of what better looks like. Everyone needs to be able to explain how they know that their efforts are moving the project forward for people to be able to work together. Projects that need something as extreme as a legacy modernization effort have no shortage of problems to solve. By defining success, you keep the finish line from moving.

In the next chapter, I will explain how to maintain software on a day-to-day basis to avoid having to run legacy modernizations in the first place. The finish line of a modernization effort need not be that everything is fixed and the technology is now perfect. I have yet to encounter a system that could be described that way, and I have worked for organizations as young as six months and as old as 200 years. All technology is imperfect, so the goal of legacy modernization should not be restoring mythical perfection but bringing the system to a state where it is possible to maintain modern best practices around security, stability, and availability.

10

FUTURE-PROOFING

The best way to complete a modernization project is by ensuring that you won't have to go through the whole process again in a few years. Future-proofing isn't about preventing mistakes; it's about knowing how to maintain and evolve technology gradually.

Two types of problems will cause us to rethink a working system as it ages. The first are usage changes. The second are deteriorations. *Scaling challenges* are the change in usage type: we have more traffic or a different type of traffic from what we had before. Maybe more people are using the system than were before, or we've added a bunch of features that over time have changed the purpose for which people are using the technology.

Usage changes do not have a constant pace and are, therefore, hard to predict. A system might never have scaling challenges. A system can reach a certain level of usage and never go any further. Or it can double or triple in size in a brief period. Or it can slowly increase in scale for years. What scaling challenges will look like if they do happen will depend on a number of factors. Because changes to the system's usage are hard to anticipate, they are hard to normalize. This is an advantage. When we normalize something, we stop thinking about it, stop factoring it into our decisions, and sometimes even forget it exists.

Deteriorations, on the other hand, are inevitable. They represent a natural linear progression toward an unavoidable end state. Other factors may speed them up or slow them down, but eventually, we know what the final outcome will be. For example, no changes in usage were going to eliminate the 9th of September from the calendar year of 1999. It was going to happen at some point, regardless of the system behavior of the machines that were programmed to use 9/9/99 as a null value assigned to columns when the date was missing.

Memory leaks are another good example of this kind of change. System usage might influence exactly when the leak creates a major problem, but low system usage will not change the fact that a memory leak exists that will eventually be a problem. The only way to escape the problem is to fix it.

Hardware lifecycles are another example. Eventually chips, disks, and circuit boards all fail and have to be replaced.

These kinds of deteriorations are dangerous because people forget about them. For a long time, their effects go unnoticed, until one day they finally and completely break. If the organization is particularly unlucky, the problem is deeply embedded in the system, and it's not immediately clear what has even broken in the first place.

Consider, for example, Y2K. An alarming number of computer programs were designed with a two-digit year, which became a problem in the year 2000 when the missing first two digits were different from what the program assumed they were. Most technical people know the Y2K story, but did you know that Y2K wasn't the first short-sighted programming mistake of this nature? Nor will it be the last.

Time

It's unbelievable how often software engineers have screwed up time in programs. In the 1960s, some programs had only one-digit years.

The TOPS-10 operating system had only enough bits to represent dates between January 1, 1964, and January 4, 1975. Engineers patched this problem, adding three more bits so that TOPS-10 could represent dates up to February 1, 2052, but they took those bits from existing data structures, thinking they were unused. It turns out that some programs on TOPS-10 had already repurposed those areas of storage, which led to some wonky bugs.[1]

How much storage should be dedicated to dates is a constant problem. It would be unwise and impractical to allocate unlimited storage for time, and yet any amount of storage eventually will run out. Programmers must decide how many years will pass before the idea that their program will still be functioning seems unlikely. At least in the early days of computers, the tendency was to underestimate the lifecycle of software. It's easy for a functioning piece of software to remain in place for 10, 20, 30 years, or more. But in the early days of computing, two or three decades seemed like a long time. If time was given only enough space to reach 1975, the fix might carry it over to 1986. Certain operating systems in 1989 programmed limits to reach maturity in 1997—and so on, and on, and on.

These programs are still with us, and we haven't reached all of their maturity dates just yet. In 2028, a date format created by the World Computer Corporation will reach its storage limit, and we have no idea whether any existing systems use it. Of greater concern is the year 2038 when Unix's 32-bit dates reach their limit. While most modern Unix implementations have switched to 64-bit dates instead, the Network Time Protocol's (NTP) 32-bit date components will overflow on February 7, 2036, giving us a potential preview. NTP handles syncing the clocks of computers that talk with each other over the internet. Computer clocks that are too badly out of sync—typically five minutes or more— have trouble creating secure connections. This requirement goes back to

---

[1.] Dan Hoey, "Software Alert: DATE-86," *Australian Unix Systems User Group Newsletter* 6, no. 4 (January 1986), 37.

MIT's Kerberos version 5 spec in 2005, which used time to keep attackers from resetting their clocks to continue using expired tickets.

We don't know what kinds of problems NTP and Unix rollovers will cause. Most computers are probably long upgraded and will be unaffected. With any luck, the 2038 milestone will pass us by with little fanfare, just as Y2K did before it. But time bugs don't need to trigger global meltdowns to have dramatic and expensive impacts. Past time bugs have temporarily cleared pension funds, messed with text messages, crashed video games, and disabled parking meters. In 2010, 20 million chip and PIN bank cards became unusable in Germany thanks to a time bug.[2] In 2013, NASA lost control of the $330 million Deep Impact probe thanks to a time bug similar to the 2038 issue.

Time bugs are tricky because they detonate decades, or sometimes centuries, after they were introduced. IBM mainframes built in the 1970s reach a rollover point on September 18, 2042. Some Texas Instruments calculators do not accept dates beyond December 31, 2049. Some Nokia phones accept dates only up to December 31, 2079. Several programming languages and frameworks use timestamp objects that overflow on April 11, 2262.

It's not that programmers don't know these bugs exist. It's just hard to imagine the technology of today sticking around until 2262. At the same time, people who were programming room-sized mainframes in the 1960s never thought their code would last for decades, but we now know programs this old are still in production. By the time the year 2000 came around, that old software (and sometimes the machines that came with it) had not only not been retired but was also being maintained by technologists two or three generations divorced from its creation.

Resolving time bugs is usually fairly straightforward—when we know about them. The problem is we tend to forget that they're approaching.

---

2 James Wilson, "German Bank Cards Hit by '2010' Bug," *Financial Times*, January 5, 2010.

We have already seen systems fail thanks to the 2038 bug. Programs in financial institutions that must calculate out interest payments 20 or 30 years into the future act like early warning detection systems for these types of errors. Still, organizations must know the state of their legacy systems (in other words, whether they've been patched) and be aware that these incidents are happening.

Unescapable Migrations

Future-proofing systems does not mean building them so that you never have to redesign them or migrate them. That is impossible. It means building and, more important, *maintaining* to avoid a lengthy modernization project where normal operations have to be reorganized to make progress. The secret to future-proofing is making migrations and redesigns normal routines that don't require heavy lifting.

Most modern engineering organizations already know how to do this with usage changes—they monitor for increased activity and scale infrastructure up or down as needed. If given proper time and prioritization, they will refactor and redesign components of the system to better reflect the most likely long-term usage patterns. Making updates to the system early and often is just a matter of discipline. Those that neglect to devote a little bit of time to cleaning their technical debt will be forced into cumbersome and risky legacy modernization efforts instead.

One of my favorite metaphors for setting a cadence for early and often updates comes from the podcast *Legacy Code Rocks* (*https://www.legacycode.rocks/*). Launching a new feature is like having a house party. The more house parties you have in your house before you clean things up, the worse condition your house will be in. Although there isn't a hard-and-fast rule here that will work for everyone, automatically scheduling some time to reevaluate usage changes and technical debt after every *n* feature launches will normalize the process of updating the system in ways that will ensure its long-term health. When people associate refactoring and necessary migrations with a system somehow being built wrong or breaking, they will put off doing them until things are falling apart. When the process of managing these changes is part of the routine, like getting a haircut or changing the oil in your car, the system can be future-proofed by gradually modernizing it.

Deteriorations require a different tact. Sometimes they can be monitored. As batteries age, for example, their performance slides in a way that can be captured and tracked. Some deteriorations are more sudden. Time bugs don't give any warning before they explode. If the organization has forgotten about it, there's nothing to monitor.

It would be naive to say that you should never build a deteriorating change into your system; those issues are often unavoidable. The mistake is assuming it is not possible that the system will still be operational when the issue matures. Technology has a way of extending its life for much longer than people realize. Some of the control panels for switches on the New York City subway date back to the 1930s. The Salisbury cathedral clock started running in 1368. There's a lightbulb over Livermore California's Fire Station 6 that has been on since 1901. All around the world, our day-to-day lives are governed by machines long past their assumed expiration dates.

Instead, managing deteriorations comes down to these two practices:

- If you're introducing something that will deteriorate, build it to fail gracefully.

- Shorten the time between upgrades so that people have plenty of practice doing them.

Failing Gracefully

The reason Y2K and similar bugs do not trigger the end of human civilization is because they do not impact every system affected by them with uniform intensity. There is a lot of variation in how different machines, different programming languages, and different software will handle the same problem. Some systems will panic; some will simply move on. Whether it is better for the system to panic and crash or to ignore the issue and move on largely depends on whether the failure is in the critical path of a transaction.

Failing gracefully does not always mean the system avoids crashing. If a bug breaks a daily batch job calculating accrued interest on bank accounts, the system recovering from the error by defaulting to zero and moving on is not failing gracefully. That's an outcome that if allowed to fail silently will upset a lot of people very quickly, whereas a panic would alert the engineering team immediately to the problem so it could be resolved and the batch job rerun.

How close is the error to a user interface? If the error is something potentially triggered by user input, failing gracefully means catching the error and logging the event but ultimately directing the user to try again with a useful message explaining the problem.

Will the error block other independent processes? Why is it blocking other processes? Blocking implies shared resources, which would suggest that processes are not as independent as originally thought. For truly independent processes, it is probably okay to log the error but ultimately let the system move on.

Is the error in one step of a larger algorithm? If so, you likely have no choice but to trigger a panic. If you could eliminate a step in a multistep process and not affect the final outcome, you should probably rethink whether those steps are necessary.

Will the error corrupt data? In most cases, bad data is worse than no data. If a certain error is likely to corrupt data, you must panic upon the error so the problem can be resolved.

These are good things to consider when programming in unavoidable deteriorations. This thought exercise is less useful when you don't know that you have no choice but to program in a potential bug. You can't know what you don't know.

But, it's worthwhile to take some time to consider how your software would handle issues like the date being 20 years off, time moving backward for a second, numbers appearing that are technically impossible (like 11:59:60 PM), or storage drives suddenly disappearing.

When in doubt, default to panicking. It's more important that errors get noticed so that they can be resolved.

Less Time Between Upgrades, Not More

A few years ago, I got one of those cheesy letter boards for my kitchen—you know, the ones you put inspirational messages on like "Live life in full bloom" or "Love makes this house a home." Except, mine says "The truth is counterintuitive." Our gut instinct with deteriorations is to push them as far back as possible if we cannot eliminate them altogether. Personally, I feel this is a mistake. I know from experience that the more often engineers have to do things, the better they get at doing them, and the more likely they are to remember that they need to be done and plan accordingly.

For example, in 2019 there were two important time bugs. The first was a rollover of GPS's epoch; the second was a leap second.

The GPS rollover is a problem identical to the time bugs already described. GPS represents weeks in a storage block of 10 bytes. That means it can store up to 1024 values, and 1024 weeks is 19.7 years. As with Y2K, when GPS gets to week number 1025, it resets to zero, and the computer has no way of knowing that it shouldn't backdate everything by 20 years.

This had happened only once before, in 1999. Although commercial GPS has been available since the 1980s, it had not really caught on by 1999. The chips that powered the receiver were too expensive, and their convenience would not be realized until computers became fast enough to overlay that data with calculations determining routes or associating physical landmarks with their coordinates. As the helpful bits of GPS were not yet market-ready, consumers were more sensitive to the privacy concerns of the technology. In 1997, employees for United Parcel Service (UPS) famously went on strike after UPS tried to install GPS receivers in all of their trucks.

So, the impacts of the first GPS rollover were minor, because GPS was not popular. By 2019, however, the world was a completely different place. Twenty years is a long time in technology. Not only were virtually all cellphones equipped with GPS chips, but any number of applications had been built on top of GPS.

As it turns out, people replace GPS-enabled devices a lot. Mobile app updates for many users are seamless and automatic. We are so used to getting new phones every two or three years that the rollover of 2019 was mainly uneventful. Users with older-model mobile phones experienced some problems but were encouraged to buy new phones from their vendors instead.

The second time bug of 2019, a leap second, went a slightly different way. A leap second is exactly what it sounds like: an extra second tacked on to the year to keep computer clocks in sync with the solar cycle. Unlike a leap year, leap seconds are not predictable. How many seconds between sun up and sun down depends on the earth's rotational speed, which is changing. Different forces push the earth to speed up, and others push the earth to slow down.

Here's a fun fact: one of the many forces changing the speed of the earth's rotation is climate change. Ice weighs down the land masses on Earth, and when it melts, those land masses start to drift up toward the poles. This makes the earth spin faster and days fractions of a second shorter.

There have been 28 leap seconds between 1972 and 2020, but as some forces slow the earth down and some forces speed it up, there can be significant gaps between years with leap seconds. After the leap second in 1999, it was six years before another was needed. There were no leap seconds between 2009 and 2012. There was a leap second in both 2015 and 2016, but nothing in the next three years.

Leap seconds are never fun, but if the reports of problems experienced during each recent leap second can be considered comprehensive, they are worse after a long gap than they would be otherwise. Even gaps as short as three years are long enough for new technologies either to be developed or to get much more traction than they had before. Abstractions and assumptions are made, and they settle into working systems and then are forgotten.

The industries around cloud computing and smartphones started to grow just as a multiyear gap in leap seconds was approaching. By the time the next leap second event occurred, huge platforms were running on technologies that had not existed during the last one. These technologies were built by engineers who may not even have been familiar with the concept of a leap second in the first place. Some service owners failed to patch updates to manage the leap second in a timely manner. Reddit, Gawker Media, Mozilla, and Qantas Airways all experienced problems.

This was followed by another multiyear gap before the leap second of 2015 created issues for Twitter, Instagram, Pinterest, Netflix, Amazon, and Beats 1 (now Apple Music 1). By comparison, 2016's leap second went out with a whimper. With just a six-month gap, it seems to have triggered problems only in a small number of machines across CloudFlare's 102 data centers.

And the 2019 leap second at the end of another multiyear gap? It cancelled more than 400 flights when Collins Aerospace's Automatic dependent surveillance–broadcast (ADS–B) system failed to adjust correctly. ADS–B was not new, but the FAA had released a rule requiring it on planes by 2020, so its adoption was much greater than it had been at the time of the previous leap second.

As a general rule, we get better at dealing with problems the more often we have to deal with them. The longer the gap between the maturity date of deteriorations, the more likely knowledge has been lost and critical functionality has been built without taking the inevitable into account. Although the GPS rollover came at the end of a 20-year gap, it benefited from the accelerated upgrade cycle of devices most likely to be affected. Few people have 20-year-old cellphones or tablets. Leap seconds, on the other hand, have pretty consistently caused chaos when there's a gap between the current one and the last one.

Some deteriorations have such short gaps at scale and don't need the organization to do any extra meddling. For example, the average storage drive has a lifespan of three to five years. If you have one drive—for example, the one in your computer—you can mitigate the risks of this inevitable failure by regularly backing things up and just replacing the computer when the drive ultimately fails.

If you are running a data center, you need a strategy to keep drive failure from crippling operations. You need to back up regularly and restore almost instantaneously. That might seem like a huge engineering challenge, but the architecture to create such resilience is built in to the scale. Data centers don't have just a few hard drives and three- to five-year gaps when they need to be replaced. Data centers often have thousands to hundreds of thousands of drives that are failing *constantly*. In 2008, Google announced it had sorted a petabyte of data in six hours with 4,000 computers using 48,000 storage drives. A single run always resulted in at least one of the 48,000 drives dying.[3] A formal study of the issue done at about the same time pegged the annual drive failure rate at 3 percent.[4] At 3 percent failure rate, once you get into the hundreds of thousands of drives, you start seeing multiple drives failing every day.

While no one would argue that drive failures are pleasant, they do not trigger outages once data centers reach a scale where handling drive failure is a regular occurrence. So rather than lengthening the period

---

[3] Grzegorz Czajkowski, "Sorting 1PB with MapReduce," *Google Blog*, November 21, 2008, *https://googleblog.blogspot.com/2008/11/sorting-1pb-with-mapreduce.html*.

[4] Eduardo Pinheiro, Wolf-Dietrich Weber, and Luiz Andre Barroso, "Failure Trends in a Large Disk Drive Population," *Proceedings of the 5th USENIX Conference on File and Storage Technologies*, February 2007.

between inevitable changes, it might be better to shorten it to ensure engineering teams are building with the assumption of the inevitable at the forefront of their thoughts and that the teams that would have to resolve the issue understand what to do.

A Word of Caution About Automation

The second solution people gravitate to if a deteriorating change cannot be eliminated altogether is to automate its resolution. In some cases, this kind of automation adds a lot of value with relatively little risk. For example, failing regularly to renew TLS/SSL certificates could cause an entire system to grind to a halt suddenly and without warning. Automating the process of renewing them means the certificates themselves can have shorter lifespans, which increases the security benefit of using them.

The main thing to consider when thinking about automating a problem away is this: If the automation fails, will it be clear what has gone wrong? In most cases, expired TLS/SSL certificates trigger obvious alerts. Either the connection is refused, at which point the validity of the certificate should be on the checklist of likely culprits, or the user receives a warning that the connection is insecure.

Automation is more problematic when it obscures or otherwise encourages engineers to forget what the system is actually doing under the hood. Once that knowledge is lost, nothing built on top of those automated activities will include fail-safes in case of automation failure. The automated tasks become part of the platform, which is fine if the engineers in charge of the platform are aware of them and take responsibility for them.

Few programmers consider what would happen should garbage collection suddenly fail to execute correctly. Memory management used to be a critical part of programming, but now the responsibility is largely automated away. This works because the concern is always top of mind for software engineers who develop programming languages that have automated garbage collection.

In other words, automation is beneficial when it's clear who is responsible for the automation working in the first place and when failure states give users enough information to understand how they should triage the issue. Automation that encourages people to forget about it creates responsibility gaps. Automation that fails either silently or with unclear error messages at best wastes a lot of valuable engineering time and at worst triggers unpredictable and dangerous side effects.

Building Something Wrong the Correct Way

Throughout this book and in this chapter especially, the message has been don't build for scale before you have scale. Build something that you will have to redesign later, even if that means building a monolith to start. Build something wrong and update it often.

The secret to building technology "wrong" but in the correct way is to understand that successful complex systems are made up of stable simple systems. Before your system can be scaled with practical approaches, like load balancers, mesh networks, queues, and other trappings of distributive computing, the simple systems have to be stable and performant. Disaster comes from trying to build complex systems right away and neglecting the foundation with which all system behavior—planned and unexpected—will be determined.

A good way to estimate how much complexity your system can handle is to ask yourself: How large is the team for this? Each additional layer of complexity will require a monitoring strategy and ultimately human beings to interpret what the monitors are telling them. Figure a minimum of three people per service. For the purposes of this discussion, a service is a subsystem that has its own repository of code (although Google famously keeps all its source code in a monolith repository), has dedicated resources (either VMs or separate containers), and is assumed to be loosely coupled from other components of the system.

The minimum on-call rotation is six people. So, a large service with a team of six can have a separate on-call rotation, or two small services can share a rotation among their teams. People can, of course, be on multiple teams, or the same team can run multiple services, but a person cannot be well versed in an infinite number of topics, so for every additional service, expect the level of expertise to be cut in half. In general, I prefer engineers not take on more than two services, but I will make exceptions when services are related.

I lay out these restrictions only to give you a framework from which to think about the capacity of the human beings on which your system relies to future-proof it. You can change the exact numbers to fit what you think is realistic if you like. The tendency among engineers is to build with an eye toward infinite scale. Lots of teams model their systems after white papers from Google or Amazon when they do not have the team to maintain a Google or an Amazon. What the human resources on a team can support is the upper bound on the level of system complexity. Inevitably the team will grow, the usage of the system will grow, and many of these architectural decisions will have to be revised. That's fine.

Here's an example: Service A needs to send data to Service B. The team maintaining the complete system has about 11 people on it. Four people are on operations, maintaining the servers and building tooling to help enforce standards. Four people are on the data science team, designing models and writing the code to implement them, and the remaining three people build the web services. That three-person team maintains Service B but also another service elsewhere in the system. The data science team maintains Service A, but also two other services.

Both of those teams are a bit overloaded for their staffing levels, but the usage of the system is low, so the pressure isn't too great.

So, how should Service A talk to Service B?

The first suggestion is to set up a message queue so that communication between A and B is decoupled and resilient. That would be the most scalable solution, but it would also require someone to set up the message queue and the workers, monitor them, and respond when something goes wrong. Which team is responsible for that? Cynical engineers will probably say operations. This is usually what happens when teams cannot support what they are building. Certain parts of the system get abandoned, and the only people who pay attention to them are the teams that are in charge of the infrastructure itself (and usually only when something is on fire).

Although a message queue is more scalable, a simpler solution with tighter coupling would probably get better results to start. Service A could just send an HTTP request to Service B. Delegation of responsibilities on triage is built in. If the error is thrown on the Service B side, the team that owns Service B is alerted. If it's thrown on the Service A side, the team that owns Service A is alerted.

But what about network issues? It's true that networks sometimes fail, but if we assume that both of these services are hosted on a major cloud provider, the chances of a one-off network issue that causes no other problems are unlikely. Networking issues are not subtle, and they are generally a product of misconfiguration rather than gremlins.

The HTTP request solution is wrong in the correct way because migrating from an HTTP request between Service A and Service B to a message queue later is straightforward. While we are temporarily losing built-in fault tolerance and accepting a higher scaling burden, it creates a system that is easier for the current teams to maintain.

The counterexample would be if we swapped the order of the HTTP request and had Service B poll Service A for new data. While this is also less complex than a message queue, it is unnecessarily resource-intensive. Service A does not produce a constant stream of new data, and by polling Service B, it may spend hours or even days sending meaningless requests. Moving from this to a queue would require significant changes to the code. There's little value to building things wrong this way.

Feedback Loops

Another way to think about this is to sketch out how maintaining this system will create feedback loops across engineering. Thinking about how work gets done in terms of flows, delays, stocks, and goals can help clarify whether the level of work required to maintain a system of a given complexity is feasible.

Let's take another look at the question of Service A and Service B. We know we have seven people working on these two services and that each person has an eight-hour workday. Service B's team is split between that and another service, so we can assume they have a budget of four hours per service they own. With three people, that's about 12 hours per day. Service A's team is maintaining a total of three services, so they have a budget of 2.5 hours per person and 10 hours per service per day. A model like this might have the following characteristics:

STOCKS A *stock* is any element that can accrue or drain over time. The traditional example of a system model is a bathtub filling with water. The water is a stock. In this model, technical debt will accrue for each service constantly regardless of the level of work. Debt will be paid down by spending work hours. The tasks in our workweek are also a stock that our teams will burn down as they operate. That eight-hour day is also a stock. When the system is stable, the eight hours are fully spent and fully restored each day.

FLOWS A *flow* is a change that either increases or decreases a stock. In the bathtub example, the rate of water coming out of the faucet is a flow, and if the drain is open, the rate of water coming out of the bathtub is another flow. In our model, at any time, people can work more than eight hours a day, but doing so will decrease their ultimate productivity and require them to work less than eight hours a day later. We can represent this by assuming that we're borrowing the extra hours for the next day's budget. Tasks are completed by spending work hours; we might keep our model simple and say every task is worth an hour, or we might separate tasks into small, medium, and large sizes with different number-of-hours costs for each option. Spending work hours decreases the stock of technical debt or work tasks, depending on how those hours are applied.

DELAYS Good systems models acknowledge that not everything is instantaneous. *Delays* represent gaps of time in how flows respond. With our model, new work does not immediately replace old work; it is planned and assigned in one-week increments. We can view the period between each task assignment as being a delay.

FEEDBACK *Feedback loops* form when the change in stock affects the nature of the flow, either positively or negatively. In our model, when people work more than their total eight-hour budget, they lose future hours. The more hours they work, the more hours they have to borrow to maintain a stretch of eight-hour days in a row. Eventually, they have to take time off to normalize. Alternatively, they could borrow hours by spending more of their budget on Service A or Service B, but that means the other services they are responsible for will be neglected, and their technical debt will accrue unchecked.

Visually, we might represent that model like in Figure 10-1. The solid lines represent flows, and the dotted lines represent variables that influence the rate of flows.

Work hours come into the model via our schedule but are affected by a stock representing burnout. If burnout is high, work hours fall; if work hours are high, burnout rises. How much of our available work hours on any given day is devoted to tasks on one service depends on the size of our team and the number of services or projects the team is trying to maintain at the same time. The more we are able to devote to work tasks, the more we ship. When work tasks are completed, whatever extra time is left is directed to improving our technical debt.

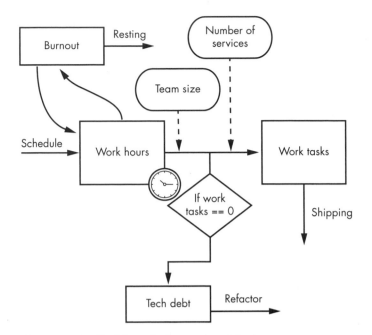

Figure 10-1: *Feedback loops in the team's workload*

Although this visual model might just look like an illustration, we can actually program it for real and use it to explore how our team manages its work in various conditions. Two tools popular with system thinkers for these kinds of models are Loopy (*https://ncase.me/loopy/*). and Insight-Maker (*https://insightmaker.com/*). Both are free and open source, and both allow you to experiment with different configurations and interactions.

For now, let's just think through a couple scenarios. Suppose we have a sprint with 24 hours of work tasks for Service A and for Service B. That shouldn't be a problem; Service A's team has a weekly capacity of 50 hours a week for Service A, and Service B's team has a weekly capacity of 60 hours a week for Service B. With 24 hours of sprint tasks, each team has plenty of extra time to burn down technical debt.

But what happens if a sprint has 70 hours of work? Service A's team could handle that if every one of the team's four people borrowed five hours that week from the next week, but the team would have no time to manage technical debt and would have only 30 hours of time for Service A the following week.

What if 70 hours of work were the norm for sprints? The teams would slowly burn out while having no ability to rethink the system design or manage their debt. The model is unstable, but we can restore equilibrium by doing one of the following:

- The team transfers ownership of one of their services to another team, giving them more hours a day to spend on their tasks for Service A or Service B.

- The team allows technical debt to accrue on one or all of their services until a service fails.

- The team works more and more until individuals burn out, at which point they become unavailable for a period of time.

One of the things that the teams might do to try to reestablish equilibrium is change the design so that the integration pattern means less work for Service A's lower-capacity team. Suppose that instead of connecting over HTTP, Service B connected directly to Service A's database to get the data it needs. Service A's team would no longer have to build an endpoint to receive requests from Service B, which means they could better balance their workload and manage their maintenance responsibilities, but the model would reach equilibrium at the expense of the quality of the overall architecture.

If you're a student of Fred Brooks's *The Mythical Man-Month*, you might object to the premise of this model. It suggests that one possible solution is to add more people to the team, and we know that software is not successfully built in man-hours. More people do not make software projects go faster.

But the point of this type of model is not to plan a road map or budget head count. It's to help people consider the engineering team as a system of interconnected parts. Bad software is unmaintained software.

Future-proofing means constantly rethinking and iterating on the existing system. People don't go into building a service thinking that they will neglect it until it's a huge liability for their organization. People fail to maintain services because they are not given the time or resources to maintain them.

If you know approximately how much work is in an average sprint and how many people are on the team, you can reason about the likelihood that a team of that size will be able to successfully maintain X number of services. If the answer is no, the design of the architecture is probably too complex for the current team.

Don't Stop the Bus

In summary, systems age in two different ways. Their usage patterns change, which require them to be scaled up and down, or the resources that back them deteriorate up to the point where they fail. Legacy modernizations themselves are anti-patterns. A healthy organization running a healthy system should be able to evolve it over time without rerouting resources to a formal modernization effort.

To achieve that healthy state, though, we have to be able to see the levels and hierarchy of the systems of systems we're building. Our technical systems are made up of smaller systems that must be stable. Our engineering team behaves as another system, establishing feedback loops that determine how much time and energy they can spend on the upgrades necessary to evolve a technology. The engineering system and the technical system are not separate from each other.

I once had a senior executive tell me, "You're right about the seriousness of this security vulnerability, Marianne, but we can't stop the bus." What he meant by this was that he didn't want to devote resources to fixing it because he was worried it would slow down new development. He was right, but he was right only because the organization had been ignoring the problem in question for two or three years. Had they addressed it when it was discovered, they could have done so with minimum investment. Instead, the problem multiplied as engineers copied the bad code into other systems and built more things on top of it. They had a choice: slow down the bus or wait for the wheels to fall off the bus.

Organizations choose to keep the bus moving as fast as possible because they can't see all the feedback loops. Shipping new code gets attention, while technical debt accrues silently and without fanfare. It's not the age of a system that causes it to fail, but the pressure of what the organization has forgotten about it slowly building toward an explosion.

CONCLUSION

The hard part about legacy modernization is the system around the system. The organization, its communication structures, its politics, and its incentives are all intertwined with the technical product in such a way that to move the product, you must do it by turning the gears of this other, complex, undocumented system.

Part of the reason legacy modernizations fail so often is that human beings are incentivized to mute or otherwise remove feedback loops that establish accountability. We are often unable to stop this because we insist on talking about that problem as a moral failing instead of an unconscious bias. Engineering organizations that maintain a separation between operations and development, for example, inevitably find that their development teams design solutions so that when they go wrong, they impact the operations team first and most severely. Meanwhile, their operations team builds processes that throw barriers in front of development, passing the negative consequences of that to those teams. These are both examples of muted feedback loops. The implementers of a decision cannot feel the impacts of their decisions as directly as some other group.

One of the reasons the DevOps and SRE movements have had such a beneficial effect on software development is that they seek to re-establish accountability. If product engineering teams play a role in running and maintaining their own infrastructure, they are the ones who feel the impact of their own decisions. When they build something that doesn't scale, they are the ones who are awakened at 3 AM with a page. Making software engineers responsible for the health of their infrastructure instead of a separate operations team unmutes the feedback loop.

But anyone who has ever tried to run an SRE or DevOps team will tell you that maintaining the expectation that product engineering teams should be responsible for their infrastructure is easier said than done. There will always be a need for specialists on the infrastructure side of things—either because the organization is running its own data centers and needs the hardware expertise or because the tools that engineers interact with to maintain their infrastructure need themselves to be maintained—and, therefore, there is always someone to dump responsibilities on.

People do not mute feedback loops because they do not care. They mute feedback loops because human beings can hold only so much information in their minds at one point. Keeping a feedback loop open means listening for information from it, which means first considering what information might come back and how to interpret it. Developers mute operations because they usually do not understand the details of how infrastructure works. Engineers typically mute the feedback loop from the business side of the organization, because that feedback is delivered in metrics they're not trained on and struggle to extract insight from. Each group is capable of learning the language of the other, but how many disciplines should a single person be expected to master to do her job? When running a system, engineers must consider resource usage, capacity projections, test coverage, inheritance structure, lines of code, and more. Is it any wonder most restrict their scope to the massive technical complexity directly relevant to what their job actually is?

A high-functioning organization cannot have all feedback loops open all the time. It must decide which loops have the biggest impact on operational excellence. Throughout this book, I have emphasized thinking about modernization projects not in terms of technical correctness but in terms of value add because it re-establishes the most important feedback loop: Is the technology serving the needs of its users?

Meetings, reports, and dialogues are the least efficient feedback loops. Feedback loops are most effective when the operator *feels* the impact, rather than just hearing about it. That's because people are naturally inclined to misinterpret information to suit what they already want to believe. It is more difficult to do that when the feedback is delivered in the form of inconvenience, disruption, interruptions, and additional work.

Nevertheless, since we cannot have all feedback loops open all the time, traditional communication can help fill in where impacts are not serious enough to warrant an open loop. Designing a modernization effort is about iteration, and iteration is about feedback. Therefore, the real challenge of legacy modernization is not the technical tasks, but making sure the feedback loops are open in the critical places and communication is orderly everywhere else.

As a general rule, the discretion to make decisions should be delegated to the people who must implement those decisions. If you are not contributing code or being woken up in the middle of the night to answer a page, have the good sense to remember that no matter how important your job is, you are not the implementor. You do not operate the system, but you can find the operators and make sure they have the air cover they need to be successful. Empower the operators.

It should go without saying that this requires trust. Teams are ultimately governed by trust. Leaders of large organizations do not like hearing this, because it means they will be held accountable for outcomes that are beyond their control. It is easier to cling to a popular strategy that offers guarantees. That way, if it fails, it can be passed off as a freak occurrence no leader could have prevented. There are no silver bullets with legacy modernization; every technique in this book could fail under the wrong conditions. I've done my best to describe the right conditions, and the vulnerabilities of each approach, but I am limited by my knowledge and experience, which are not (and never will be) infinite. The person in the best position to find a working strategy is the person on the ground watching the gears of the system turn.

Dealing with this reality gets easier when you accept failure. Failure is inevitable when attempting to change complex systems in production. There are too many moving parts, too many unknowns, and too much that needs to be fixed. Getting every single decision right is impossible. Modern engineering teams use stats like service level objectives, error budgets, and mean time to recovery to move the emphasis away from avoiding failure and toward recovering quickly. Don't forget: a perfect record can always be broken, but resilience is an accomplishment that lasts. Embracing failure as an organization diminishes the risk of empowering the operator and gets better performance from engineers.

We cannot completely eliminate failure, because there's a level of complexity where a single person—no matter how intelligent—cannot comprehend the full system. With legacy systems, we have an additional complication in the fact that some context of the system has been lost. Requirements, assumptions, and the technical limitations of the time are all undocumented. There may be abstractions buried in the platform that trip us up. Modernization teams need to rediscover the requirements and assumptions of the original system and update them for the new system, but there are limitations on how much understanding even the best modernization team can excavate. Ultimately, old software cannot be used as a specification for a new version.

Technology, at its core, is an artifact of human thought. So when modernizing old technology, what humans think matters quite a lot. Software engineers are smart, but they fall victim to trends and fads the same as any other profession. Pay attention to how they are incentivized. What earns them the acknowledgment of their peers? What gets people seen is what they will ultimately prioritize, even if those behaviors are in open conflict with the official instructions they receive from management. Technology advances in cycles with old paradigms constantly being dusted off to capture neglected segments of the market. Newer is not necessarily better. Good technology isn't about having the most modern, most scalable, fastest, or most secure implementation; it's about serving the needs of the user.

But, we also want a world where software engineers strive to make technology faster, better, and more secure. The only way we get both technology that serves the user and strives to improve continuously is by defining success up front. What does it mean to bring value, and how do we know when value has increased?

In the end, technology is never finished being built. The legacy modernization projects of today were the finished systems of yesterday. Computer systems cannot be expected to go unchanged for decades, because rarely is a computer isolated from the outside world. The inputs will change, the output methods will change, the networks and protocols will change, and the program that doesn't change becomes a time bomb.

The best way to handle legacy modernization projects is not to need them in the first place. If the appropriate time and resources are budgeted for it, systems can be maintained in such a way that they evolve with the industry. The organizations that accomplish this ultimately understand that the organization's scale is the upper bound of system complexity. Systems that are more complex than the team responsible for them can maintain are neglected and eventually fall apart.

To most software engineers, legacy systems may seem like torturous dead-end work, but the reality is systems that are not used get turned off. Working on legacy systems means working on some of the most critical systems that exist—computers that govern millions of people's lives in enumerable ways. This is not the work of technical janitors, but battlefield surgeons. It has been the greatest honor to serve among them.

INDEX